F.V.

WITHDRAWN

St. Louis Community
College

Forest Park
Florissant Valley
Meramec

Instructional Resources
St. Louis, Missouri

MAYA ANGELOU

MAYA ANGELOU

A Critical Companion

Mary Jane Lupton

CRITICAL COMPANIONS TO POPULAR CONTEMPORARY WRITERS
Kathleen Gregory Klein, Series Editor

Greenwood Press
Westport, Connecticut • London

Library of Congress Cataloging-in-Publication Data

Lupton, Mary Jane
    Maya Angelou : a critical companion / Mary Jane Lupton.
       p. cm.—(Critical companions to popular contemporary
  writers, ISSN 1082–4979)
    Includes bibliographical references and index.
    ISBN 0–313–30325–8 (alk. paper)
    1. Angelou, Maya—Criticism and interpretation. I. Title.
  II. Series.
  PS3551.N464L86   1998
  818'.5409—dc21   98–17489

British Library Cataloguing in Publication Data is available.

Library of Congress Catalog Card Number: 98–17489
ISBN: 0–313–30325–8
ISSN: 1082–4979

First published in 1998

Greenwood Press, 88 Post Road West, Westport, CT 06881
An imprint of Greenwood Publishing Group, Inc.

Printed in the United States of America

∞

The paper used in this book complies with the
Permanent Paper Standard issued by the National
Information Standards Organization (Z39.48–1984).

10 9 8 7 6 5 4 3 2

Copyright Acknowledgments

The author and the publisher gratefully acknowledge permission for use of material
from Mary Jane Lupton's interview ("Talking with an Icon") with Maya Angelou on
June 16, 1997 and the publicity photo of Maya Angelou taken by Steve Dunwell.

In loving memory
of my friend and mentor,
Harry L. Jones
(1924–1997),
Professor Emeritus, Morgan State University

ADVISORY BOARD

Contents

Series Foreword

The authors who appear in the series Critical Companions to Popular Contemporary Writers are all best-selling writers. They do not simply have one successful novel, but a string of them. Fans, critics, and specialist readers eagerly anticipate their next book. For some, high cash advances and breakthrough sales figures are automatic; movie deals often follow. Some writers become household names, recognized by almost everyone.

But their novels are read one by one. Each reader chooses to start and, more importantly, to finish a book because of what she or he finds there. The real test of a novel is in the satisfaction its readers experience. This series acknowledges the extraordinary involvement of readers and writers in creating a best-seller.

The authors included in this series were chosen by an Advisory Board composed of high school English teachers and high school and public librarians. They ranked a list of best-selling writers according to their popularity among different groups of readers. For the first series, writers in the top-ranked group who had received no book-length, academic, literary analysis (or none in at least the past ten years) were chosen. Because of this selection method, Critical Companions to Popular Contemporary Writers meets a need that is being addressed nowhere else. The success of these volumes as reported by reviewers, librarians, and teachers led to an expansion of the series mandate to include some writers with wide critical attention—Toni Morrison, John Irving, and Maya Angelou, for example—to extend the usefulness of the series.

The volumes in the series are written by scholars with particular expertise in analyzing popular fiction. These specialists add an academic focus to the popular success that these writers already enjoy.

The series is designed to appeal to a wide range of readers. The general reading public will find explanations for the appeal of these well-known writers. Fans will find biographical and fictional questions answered. Students will find literary analysis, discussions of fictional genres, carefully organized introductions to new ways of reading the novels, and bibliographies for additional research. Whether browsing through the book for pleasure or using it for an assignment, readers will find that the most recent novels of the authors are included.

Each volume begins with a biographical chapter drawing on published information, autobiographies or memoirs, prior interviews, and, in some cases, interviews given especially for this series. A chapter on literary history and genres describes how the author's work fits into a larger literary context. The following chapters analyze the writer's most important, most popular, and most recent novels in detail. Each chapter focuses on one or more novels. This approach, suggested by the Advisory Board as the most useful to student research, allows for an in-depth analysis of the writer's fiction. Close and careful readings with numerous examples show readers exactly how the novels work. These chapters are organized around three central elements: plot development (how the story line moves forward), character development (what the reader knows of the important figures), and theme (the significant ideas of the novel). Chapters may also include sections on generic conventions (how the novel is similar to or different from others in its same category of science fiction, fantasy, thriller, etc.), narrative point of view (who tells the story and how), symbols and literary language, and historical or social context. Each chapter ends with an "alternative reading" of the novel. The volume concludes with a primary and secondary bibliography, including reviews.

The alternative readings are a unique feature of this series. By demonstrating a particular way of reading each novel, they provide a clear example of how a specific perspective can reveal important aspects of the book. In the alternative reading sections, one contemporary literary theory—way of reading, such as feminist criticism, Marxism, new historicism, deconstruction, or Jungian psychological critique—is defined in brief, easily comprehensible language. That definition is then applied to the novel to highlight specific features that might go unnoticed or be understood differently in a more general reading. Each volume defines two or three specific theories, making them part of the reader's understanding of how diverse meanings may be constructed from a single novel.

Taken collectively, the volumes in the Critical Companions to Popular Contemporary Writers series provide a wide-ranging investigation of the complexities of current best-selling fiction. By treating these novels seriously as both literary works and publishing successes, the series demonstrates the potential of popular literature in contemporary culture.

Kathleen Gregory Klein
Southern Connecticut State University

Acknowledgments

Without the support of Dolly A. McPherson, professor of English at Wake Forest University, this book might not have been realized. I met Professor McPherson at a conference of the Mid-Atlantic Writers' Association held in Baltimore in 1990. Her book, *Order Out of Chaos*, published in that same year, was the first book-length study of Angelou's autobiographical works. McPherson, a life-long personal friend of Angelou's, has supported my work since that conference and offered assistance on numerous occasions. Through her, Maya Angelou became aware of my interest in her autobiographies. Through her, I was finally successful in arranging an interview with Angelou.

I am deeply grateful to Maya Angelou for her writings, her vitality, and her kindness. I thank her for being so gracious to me and my husband, Kenneth H. Baldwin, on the night of June 16, 1997.

My husband, chair of the English department at the University of Maryland, Baltimore County, though extremely busy, still had the time to offer substantial support: counting words and citations at several stages in the manuscript; shopping for groceries; dealing with computer repairs; checking the Internet; driving me to Winston-Salem. I am grateful for his love, reassurance, and tolerance, especially during the final three months of this project.

To my daughters and their families—Julia on the West Coast and Ellen on the East—I am grateful for the phone calls, the questions, the encouragement. It was Julia's enthusiasm for the Angelou project that sparked my involvement and Ellen who kept me sound by taking me to Barcelona for five days in October 1997.

Of the friends who encouraged me in writing this book, I am especially grateful to Aimee Wiest. Since we first met in the early 1970s, Aimee has always affectionately supported my writing. She was with me during my first exhilarating, but brief meeting with Maya Angelou in 1995, following her lecture at Towson State University. Aimee, sensing my hesitation at the prearranged interview, literally pushed me into Angelou's waiting limousine.

Many friends, colleagues, and graduate students at Morgan State University have contributed to this project, among them John Clarke, Eugenia Collier, Jennifer Kreshtool, Linda Meyers, Margaret Reid, Valerie Sedlak, Ella Stevens, and Minnie Washington; and reference librarian Elaine Tsubota. I am also grateful to my students in English 102, who for almost a decade have been writing their research papers on *I Know Why the Caged Bird Sings*, sharing their insights and anger, and forcing me to be clear about my assumptions.

I am particularly indebted to Dr. Earl Richardson, president of Morgan State University, for having generously granted me a sabbatical for the fall semester 1997 so that I could complete my study of Angelou's autobiographies.

I wish also to thank my editors at Greenwood Press, Kathleen Gregory Klein and Barbara Rader, as well as copyeditor Liz Leiba, for the clarity of their suggestions and for the special care they took in the various stages of this project.

Finally, I wish to acknowledge the following women from North Carolina: Mildred Garris and Alma M. Golden of Dr. Angelou's office at Wake Forest University; Rose Johnson, who so graciously welcomed Ken and me when we visited her aunt, Maya Angelou; Sharon E. Snow, curator at the Wake Forest Library; and Joyce Ford, whose e-mails and clippings kept me constantly informed.

The Life and Works of
Maya Angelou

Maya Angelou: A Critical Companion examines the five autobiographical volumes of noted African American writer Maya Angelou. Although all of these volumes are distinct in style and narration, they are unified through a number of repeated themes and through the developing character of the narrator. In their scope they stretch over time and place, from Arkansas to Africa, from confused child to accomplished adult. With so expansive a project, Angelou is required to de-emphasize the standard autobiographical concern for the individual and to focus on her interaction with others: with the jazz singer Billie Holiday; with the actor Godfrey Cambridge; with the African American community in Ghana; with the world leader Malcolm X.

Maya Angelou, in having created these five autobiographies, has assured herself a prominent place in American literature. She has expanded the scope of the typical one-volume book about the self, creating a saga that covers the years 1941 to 1965—from the beginnings of the Second World War to the days preceding the assassination of Malcolm X. She guides the reader through a quarter of a century of American and African American history, revealed through the point of view of a strong and affectionate black woman. By opening up the edges of her narrative, Maya Angelou, like no one before her, transcends the autobiographical tradition, enriching it with contemporary experience and female sensibility.

Information about Angelou's abundant life has been recorded in numerous interviews, journals, yearbooks, prefaces, and appendices. Often there are errors or inconsistencies among these sources—the date of her first marriage; the names of awards received; the titles of plays directed; and other details. These inconsistencies arise possibly because Angelou, in her interviews, speaks eloquently but informally about her past, with no time chart in front of her, and possibly because her interviewers are so taken by her presence that they lose sight of the smaller details. The bulk of the facts presented in this chapter derive from the sources listed in the bibliography, under the category Biographical Sources. The remaining material is taken either from Angelou's published writings or from my interview with her in June 1997.

THE ICON INTERVIEW

When I agreed to write this book, I knew it would benefit from a personal interview, itself an autobiographical form. I was privileged to have met Angelou before, very briefly, in a rather dramatic limousine encounter after a lecture she gave at Towson State University in Baltimore in 1995. A return invitation, where we might really talk, seemed improbable. Nonetheless, I began writing to her press agent. After several false starts, and with the invaluable intervention of our friend Dolly A. McPherson, Angelou granted me an overnight interview that began at 4 P.M. on June 16, 1997 and ended the next morning.

My husband, Kenneth Baldwin, drove us to Winston-Salem, North Carolina. We arrived at Maya Angelou's gated property and were greeted by Rose Johnson, who I later learned was the daughter of Maya's brother Bailey. Ms. Johnson escorted us to an enormous living room and asked us to wait.

Across the room, a forty- or fifty-foot expanse, I saw a portrait of Maya Angelou as a young woman, done on a vibrant quilt, with the center panel surrounded on all sides by what appeared to be lettering. This focal piece of art was almost as tall as the space it occupied, I would guess around twelve feet. Coming close, I read the inscription: Maya's Quilt of Life, 1989/Faith Ringgold. Faith Ringgold is an African American artist and performer, well-known for her woman-oriented sculptures such as the "Family of Women" series, done in the 1970s. Her astounding Quilt of Life was commissioned by Maya Angelou's close friend, television talk-show host Oprah Winfrey, on the occasion of Angelou's sixtieth birthday.

The multitude of words framing the portrait were taken from "Phenomenal Woman," probably Angelou's most admired poem, and from "Willie," a poem about the crippled uncle immortalized in *I Know Why the Caged Bird Sings*. In addition there were excerpts from two of her autobiographies, *The Heart of a Woman* and *I Know Why the Caged Bird Sings*.

Soon after I sat down, Angelou entered the room in a rush of floor-length electric blue, with a matching blue turban decorated with gold spangles. She graciously invited Ken to stay for the interview session, which he did—but without participating. Although the investigation of form and structure in the autobiographies was at the heart of the interview, there were numerous personal moments involving husbands, cigarettes, houses, health food, aging, family. I did not perceive Maya Angelou to be a stranger. Having read her autobiographies made me feel as if she were a high-school classmate or a favorite cousin.

It became clear, as the interview progressed, that Dr. Angelou was worried, distracted. Ominously in the background as we talked was the tragic, inexplicable burning of Betty Shabazz, prominent civil-rights worker and the widow of Malcolm X, whose apartment was set on fire by her troubled grandson. On the day of the interview Maya Angelou made arrangements to go to New York City, where she, Coretta Scott King, and other friends were planning to visit Betty Shabazz in the hospital. Sadly, Shabazz died seven days later, on Monday, June 23, 1997.

Maya Angelou: A Critical Companion has been immeasurably enhanced by the interview of June 16, 1997. The figures of Martin Luther King Jr. and Malcolm X described in the fourth and fifth volumes of the autobiography became personalized, intensified. Angelou's approach to her unique serial genre was clarified. Thanks to her direct and thoughtful responses, the text of our interview serves as a major source for this work. The document also exists separately as an interview of thirty pages titled "Talking with an Icon: An Interview with Maya Angelou." An icon is a sacred image or representation, something of special value within a culture.

I refer to my interview as "Icon" because of an amusing event that occurred when Angelou was acting in the film, *How to Make an American Quilt* (1995). Members of the cast—Anne Bancroft, Ellen Burstyn, Jean Simmons, Kate Nelligan, Lois Smith, Alfre Woodard, Winona Ryder, and of course Maya Angelou—were all sitting around when the two young actresses Winona Ryder and Alfre Woodard said their friends had asked them, "What does it feel like to work with icons?"

"We laughed so hard. So I named them the iconettes," Angelou said, barely able to suppress her laughter.

For me, it was sacred to have talked with an icon and to have luxuriated in her voice, if only for a day.

LIFE

Maya Angelou was born Marguerite Annie Johnson in St. Louis, Missouri, on April 4, 1928. Throughout the series Angelou refers to herself by a number of names. Her mother liked to call her Ritie or Baby. Her thoughtless employer, Mrs. Cullinan, called her Mary. But it was her brother Bailey who gave her the name that lasted, Maya, for "My" and "my sister" (Davis in Elliot 1989, 75).

As for her stage name, she kept Rita Johnson until her marriage to Tosh Angelos in 1952. Sometime after the three-year marriage ended in divorce she opted for a more theatrical name at the strong suggestion of her managers at the San Francisco night club, the Purple Onion (Shuker 1990, 70–71). Her new name captured the feel of her Calypso performances. That name, *Maya Angelou*, will be used consistently in this book to preserve continuity.

Maya's mother, Vivian Baxter, was a nurse and card dealer; her father, Bailey Johnson Sr., was a doorman and also a dietician or meal adviser for the navy. They had a difficult marriage that ended in divorce and in their subsequent inability to deal with their young children. When Maya was three and her brother Bailey four, their father deposited the children on a train from Long Beach, California, to Stamps, Arkansas, home of Bailey Sr.'s mother, Annie Henderson, owner and operator of a general store.

Annie met the train to take charge of two forlorn children wearing instructions on their wrists that announced their names, their point of departure, and their destination. It was in the early 1930s, during the Great Depression, an economic disaster that had its roots in the American financial system but was soon felt worldwide. Still, Annie Henderson had been able to survive because her general store sold such basic commodities as beans and flour and because she made wise and honest investments.

Angelou recounts this desolate journey and arrival in the early pages of the book that has since brought her fame, *I Know Why the Caged Bird Sings*. Published in 1970 when Angelou was forty-one, it covers her life from the age of three to the age of sixteen. *Caged Bird* is the first of five autobiographies depicting the life of this African American woman of letters. The other four are *Gather Together in My Name* (1974); *Singin' and Swingin' and Gettin' Merry Like Christmas* (1976); *The Heart of a Woman* (1981); and *All God's Children Need Traveling Shoes* (1986).

THE WOMAN IN THE BOOKS

I Know Why the Caged Bird Sings

In *Caged Bird* (1970), Angelou reconstructs her childhood as a young black girl living with her protective but stern grandmother, Annie Henderson; her Uncle Willie; and her brother Bailey Johnson. This first volume vividly recalls life in Stamps, Arkansas, with its Christian traditions and its segregated society.

When Maya was eight, her father took her and Bailey from Stamps to St. Louis to visit their mother, Vivian Baxter. It was there, in 1936, in a poorly supervised household, that Maya was seduced and raped by her mother's boyfriend, Mr. Freeman. After a brief trial Freeman was beaten to death, presumably by Maya's three uncles. Horrified that her words had caused anyone's death, Maya withdrew into a silence that the Baxters were incapable of handling. She and Bailey were returned to Annie Henderson and the community of Stamps, where for five years Maya remained mute. She was finally released from the burden of speechlessness in 1940, through her study of literature and guidance by a woman from Stamps named Mrs. Flowers.

After graduating from the eighth grade, Maya, along with her brother Bailey, moved back to California, where she gave an early sign of her enormous potential to succeed by becoming the first black streetcar conductor in San Francisco. She knew even then, from her experiences in Stamps and St. Louis, that she was black and female, someone with the cards stacked against her. "If you're black you're black. Whatever you do comes out of that. It's like being a woman. No matter what age or even sexual preference, if you're a woman you're a woman" ("Icon" 1997).

Serious problems arose for Maya in her mid-teens during a disastrous summer vacation in southern California and Mexico with her father, Bailey Sr., and his girlfriend, Dolores Stockland. Maya and Dolores had a violent relationship that ended when Dolores stabbed Maya in the arm. Maya recovered, wandered around southern California awhile, and lived in a junkyard. She then returned to Vivian Baxter, who began to establish a maternal closeness with her daughter. In 1944, when she was sixteen, Maya became pregnant after inviting a neighborhood boy to have sex with her. She gave birth to a son.

In the second and third volumes Maya generally calls her son by the name of Clyde. At the end of *Singin' and Swingin' and Gettin' Merry Like Christmas*, having recovered from his sense of abandonment, Clyde announces, "My name is Guy" (237). Guy insists on this new name and trains his friends and family to accept it. As for his surname, he keeps the name Johnson, his mother's maiden name. "He had always had that name. It's a very big and important name for us, my family" ("Icon" 1997). For the sake of clarity, Maya's son will be called "Guy" throughout this book.

Gather Together in My Name

The second volume, *Gather Together in My Name* (1974), begins in the late 1940s, after the end of the Second World War and its negative effects on black lives. It concludes several years later, after Angelou has won her own personal war against drugs, prostitution, and dependency. Angelou's negative traits in this volume are intensified by a visit to Stamps, where she and Momma (Annie) Henderson confronted their differing attitudes towards race. These attitudes proved to be irreconcilable.

Much of *Gather Together* treats the issue of mothering. When Angelou became a mother she was still a child, understandably lacking in wisdom and sophistication, without job training or advanced schooling of any sort. Nevertheless, she was able to survive through trial and error, while at the same time defining herself in terms of being a black woman.

Gather Together in My Name charts her various work experiences as she moved from job to job, trying to provide for her son and survive in a hostile economic situation. She was a Creole cook, a dancer, a dishwasher, a barmaid. Frequently these jobs were entangled with her feelings for men who tried to take advantage of her naiveté.

Angelou's confession that she had been a prostitute, that she had hidden stolen goods, and that she had almost lost her son was difficult to put into words. On the brighter side, however, in the confusion and turmoil that surrounded her, Maya had been learning how to perform professionally for live audiences. Her nightclub performances with R. L. Poole proved her to be a natural dancer; in 1952, at the age of twenty-four, she reportedly won a scholarship to study under Pearl Primus, the Trinidadian choreographer whose 1943 dance creation, "Strange Fruit," was internationally acclaimed. In *Wouldn't Take Nothing for My Journey Now* (1993), she tells about her dancing partnership with Alvin Ailey (1933–1989), the great African American performer and choreographer. Ailey brilliantly combined elements of modern dance, ballet, and West African tribal dancing. Angelou and Ailey would dress in skimpy home-made costumes and hire themselves out to the Elks and the Masons as the team of Al and Rita (*Wouldn't Take Nothing for My Journey Now* 95–98). She provides no time frame for their collaboration.

As Angelou became more in demand for her singing and dancing talents, she became more emotionally distraught in knowing that her career was in conflict with her desire to be an excellent mother. This situation, very familiar to mothers with careers, becomes the major theme of her third volume.

Singin' and Swingin' and Gettin' Merry Like Christmas

Singin' and Swingin' and Gettin' Merry Like Christmas (1976) covers an unhappy stage in Maya's development. Her dancing career improved, but with it came the anguish and isolation that resulted from being away from her son. She was also separated forever from Momma Henderson, whose death is movingly commemorated in *Singin' and Swingin'*.

Maya, now Mrs. Tosh Angelos, was married and divorced in one short, unhappy interval. Again on her own, she committed herself to the European and African tour of *Porgy and Bess*, which lasted almost two years, from 1954 to 1955. She was twenty-eight years old, with a young son whom she had left with her mother, Vivian, repeating the history of her own early childhood, when she and Bailey were sent off to Momma Henderson.

Although sending one's child to stay with his grandmother is not an uncommon solution for career women with children, the decision had unpleasant effects for Maya and Guy. According to Dolly A. McPherson, Angelou's guilt and her intense love for Guy "overshadow her other experiences" in this troubling third volume (89). At the end, in an attempt to reconcile with her unhappy son, Angelou took him with her for an engagement in Hawaii, pledging to be with him in the future.

The Heart of a Woman

The Heart of a Woman (1981) is the volume that signals Angelou's maturity. She became more certain in her mothering, now that Guy was an adolescent—although there was one near disaster with a street gang when she was performing in Chicago. Still, she had promised herself to give up major tours and found fulfillment in her New York/Brooklyn environment—as an actress, a writer, and a political organizer.

Angelou's career as an actress reached a high point in 1960, when she was offered the role of the White Queen in Jean Genet's play, *The Blacks*, a dark satire about the reversal of racial power. During the same period she was at her most politically active. Moved by a sermon delivered by Martin Luther King Jr. at a Harlem church, she and actor Godfrey Cambridge, a cast member in *The Blacks*, organized a fund-raiser called "Cabaret for Freedom." As a result of her tremendous support for Dr. King, she was appointed northern coordinator of the Southern Christian Leadership Conference (SCLC), an office she held only briefly, from 1959 to 1960.

In 1961, she met a freedom fighter from South Africa, Vusumzi Make. She fell in love with his charm, intelligence, and good looks. Although she was engaged to another man, she swept it all aside and went with Vus to London for a wedding ceremony never made legal. A few months later, she and her son joined him in Egypt.

Unhappy in the house and attending afternoon parties for the wives of African revolutionaries, Angelou acted against Vus's wishes and took a job as associate editor of the *Arab Observer*, from 1961 to 1962. Her job was not the only source of antagonism between them. Other problems included Vus's failure to manage money and his affairs with other women. The couple separated in 1962, and Angelou and her son Guy moved from the east of Africa to the west, planning to go to Liberia. But after Guy was almost killed in a car accident, she was forced to situate them in Ghana, at least until he recovered.

All God's Children Need Traveling Shoes

The fifth volume, *All God's Children Need Traveling Shoes* (1986), continues its coverage of Angelou's African journey, from 1962 to 1965, although it was not published until 1986, two decades after she returned to the United States. After Guy's car accident, stunned and despairing, Angelou settled in Accra, the capital of the West African nation of Ghana. When Guy miraculously recovered, he was able not only to attend classes at the University of Ghana, but also to move toward independence from his mother. Angelou spent the early 1960s in Accra, leaving only to join a theatrical group for a tour of two European cities, Berlin and Venice.

Throughout her stay in Accra, Angelou encountered a large number of people who affected her life and her character. A few of the most influential were fellow expatriate Julian Mayfield; the renowned scholar W.E.B. Du Bois; and black Muslim leader Malcolm X. As Angelou's commitment to people and ideas increased, she pursued the political work so crucial to her development. With her expatriate friends she organized a solidarity demonstration in 1965 in support of Martin Luther King Jr.'s March on Washington and with the same group, arranged Malcolm X's itinerary when he visited Ghana the same year. She did freelance writing for the *Ghanaian Times* and worked, with the dentist Robert Lee, as a liaison between the Ghanaian government and its African American residents.

Another matter of a political and racial nature was her quest for her African roots. She took a journey beyond the outskirts of Ghana to discover her ancestors and to find people like the Bambara, who had not abandoned their ancient customs. Angelou has received praise for her search for her origins: "Her search for roots, her involvement with the politics of her people in the United States and Africa, give her work a depth that is absent in many other such works" (Cudjoe 1990, 304).

Caught between her African ancestry and her African American nationhood, Angelou eventually decided to return to America. In 1965, in a grand celebration at the Accra airport, Angelou left for the United States, as well-wishers and Ghanaian friends witnessed her departure. She said farewell to her son, leaving him in Africa to complete his university degree. Although Angelou's tone in these final pages projects a sense of separation, it also suggests that her return to America will result in work of political and artistic value.

LOOKING AT HORROR

The events recorded in *All God's Children Need Traveling Shoes* mark the extent to what readers of her formal autobiographies can know about Angelou's life up to this point. Until such time that a sixth volume might be published, readers must rely on snippets from critics and interviewers, and from her shorter autobiographical forms such as essays and musings. When I asked during the interview what she would do in a sixth volume, she answered that "I want to be able to look at horror and not find a justification but a lesson. If I can find a lesson, I can live with it if I can put it in a place" ("Icon" 1997). She then acknowledged two particular events, one in 1965 and the other in 1968, that had evoked such horror.

When Angelou arrived at the New York airport in 1965, back from Accra and en route to San Francisco, she phoned her close friend El-Hajj Malik El-Shabazz (formerly Malcolm X). Shabazz told her he was being threatened, and he recounted a recent experience in the Lincoln Tunnel where a white man rescued him from people trying to shoot him. He asked Angelou to stay over, but she was desperate to get back to the West Coast. Three days later she was out walking in San Francisco and stopped at her aunt's house, where she got a call from a friend, who said, "Girl, why did you come home? These people are crazy. Else why would they just kill that man?" ("Icon" 1997). That man, of course, was Malcolm X, who was assassinated February 21, 1965.

Three years later, Angelou ran into her friend Martin Luther King Jr. at a gala tribute to W. E. B. Du Bois at Carnegie Hall. King approached her, saying, "Maya, I will need you again. Come back with me." King wanted her to ask the nation's black preachers to support his march against poverty by contributing one day's collection a year. He said, "Come back for one month."

Maya agreed. "Okay, I will come, I'll start the Monday after my birthday."

On her birthday, April 4, 1968, she was cooking party food when her close friend and biographer, Dolly A. McPherson, called. "Sister, have you listened to the radio? Have you listened? Don't do anything. Don't answer the phone until I get there." Dolly told her that King had been killed in Memphis ("Icon" 1997).

These are two memorable stories, two appalling moments that deeply affected Angelou on her return from Ghana, to a racially torn America, moments that would stay with her forever. In the short duration of our interview she did not have time to talk about further horrors: the assassination of civil-rights workers in the 1960s; the riots in Los Angeles, Detroit, Baltimore, and elsewhere following the death of Martin Luther King Jr.; the imprisonment of activist Angela Davis in 1970; the developing drug problem and its effect on black men, women, and children.

There are many deep scars across the face of America, scars that would be examined under a microscope were Angelou to continue her autobiographical chronicles.

As to when a sixth volume would be written, she seemed uncertain. "I will do it, I say, but when? I still have to live a little longer and learn how to extract, I have to learn it. And the only way I can learn it is living" ("Icon" 1997). She is also hesitant about ever going beyond a potential sixth volume. She told Valerie Webster: "After that it would just be writing about writing which is something I don't want to do" (1989, 180).

CLOSE CONTACTS

Rarely, in fact, does Angelou write about writing. She works best in describing her place within closely confined structures such as family, marriage, and motherhood. According to Dolly A. McPherson, the concept of family in Angelou's autobiographies must take into account the manner in which she and her brother had been displaced by their parents. Thus, the family group in the five volumes goes beyond the nuclear family and even beyond the extended family: "trust is the key to a display of kinship concerns" (*Order Out of Chaos* 14). Within this kinship pattern, Angelou's relationships with her brother and grandmother are the most important. And yet, except for a few passing references, neither remains prominent after the third volume.

Over the years, Maya has remained close to her brother Bailey, her protector and confidant in *Caged Bird*, however, her trust in him was jeopardized by his having been in prison. She was reluctant to discuss his situation with me because Bailey asked her not to. He told her, "Don't use my name in books" ("Icon" 1997). Yet, in a Lifetime Television interview with Angelou conducted by Bill Moyers in 1996, Bailey was passionate about his affection for his sister, repeatedly saying that he loved her.

Evidently, there was a wonderful alliance between Bailey and Paul Du Feu, the man Maya married in 1973. At the wedding Bailey embraced Paul and called him a brother (Davis 1989, 74), although nine years later she confessed to Marney Rich, "We are not as close as we used to be" (1989, 129).

Vivian Baxter, Maya's and Bailey's mother, remained outside the family structure in *Caged Bird*. She had willfully chosen to surrender her parental rights of the children. When Bailey Sr. took his children to St.

Louis, his former wife had little to offer her abused daughter. Maya's absent mother made her feel abandoned and victimized. It was not until Maya moved to California at the age of sixteen that she and her mother formed an enduring bond that lasted through and beyond Maya's tour of Europe in 1954. Their changed relationship is recorded in *Gather Together in My Name,* a volume that ends with Maya's return to Vivian Baxter after she realizes how close to the edge she has come, as a woman and as a mother.

Maya's love for her mother is movingly presented in "Mother and Freedom," a prose piece from her 1997 book *Even the Stars Look Lonesome.* At the end of our formal interview, Angelou took us to another room where an array of galley sheets lay on the table. In her deep and captivating voice she began to read about her love for Vivian Baxter, the mother who had let Maya go: "She stood before me, a dolled-up pretty yellow woman, seven inches shorter than my six-foot bony frame" (*Stars* 47). The piece goes back and forth, from mother to daughter to mother, ending in a chilling account of her mother's dying; this once vibrant woman "lies hooked by pale blue wires to an oxygen tank, fighting cancer for her life" (48). It is clear that Vivian Baxter, who once existed outside Angelou's family, had returned to her daughter to be freed.

It seems, though, that Maya's greatest love within her family has been for her son, Guy Johnson. Guy's presence permeates each of the books following *Caged Bird.* He was the source of her problems and the source of her joy. She is his father, his mother, his sister, his teacher. He was the child she deserted when she was a professional dancer in Europe and the young man who disappointed her terribly when he had an affair with a woman in Ghana older than she was. As McPherson has observed, "Angelou becomes all the forms of family for her child and thus provides him with the security she has craved" (1990, 15).

Learning about Guy is like trying to put together a puzzle when a lot of the pieces are missing. For example, one source writes, that Guy Johnson was "Western Airline's first black executive" (Toppman 1989, 144)—much like his mother was the first black streetcar conductor in San Francisco. In an interview with this writer, Angelou mentioned that Guy is now married for the second time. She also implied, without being specific, that he is not in good health: "My son Guy feels that he is losing quite a bit of his mobility. He sits in a wheelchair. So I am designing a large bed-sit so he won't have to come up the steps or down the steps to go to the bedroom" ("Icon" 1997).

Guy's health was a painful issue throughout the autobiographies, from his skin disease in *Singin' and Swingin'* to his broken limbs in *Traveling Shoes*. Her respectful silence concerning Guy is understandable, for his well-being is a matter close to his mother's heart. When asked about her love for her son, she said, "I'll always be a mother. That's really it. If you are really a mother you can let go. . . . Because love liberates. That's what it does. It says, I love you. Wherever you go, I love you" ("Icon" 1997).

One striking aspect of Angelou's character is her unabashed honesty in describing her ability to love, in both her books and interviews. From *Caged Bird*, where she deliberately approached a young man to prove her femininity, to *Traveling Shoes*, where she welcomed a handsome, rich African lover, Angelou is open about her heterosexual relationships. She was married at least three times—first in 1951 or 1952, to a Greek sailor; then, unofficially in 1961, to a South African militant; third, in 1973, to an English builder and writer. Marriage, Angelou told Tricia Crane in 1987, is a serious personal commitment, trivialized by our shallow, soap opera culture. "So I no longer say I've been married X amount of times because I know it will not be understood" (Crane in Elliot 1989, 177).

Angelou discusses her first two marriages in *Singin' and Swingin'* and *The Heart of a Woman*, respectively. The third marriage, to Paul Du Feu, took place in 1973, about seven years after Angelou had returned from Ghana. This relationship occurred too late to have been treated within the framework of the existing autobiographies, although she gives it considerable attention in the book of short essays, *Even the Stars Look Lonesome* (1997).

Du Feu seems to have been the most satisfying and the most supportive man in her life. A celebrity in his own right, he had formerly been married to Australian feminist Germaine Greer, author of *The Female Eunuch*, published in 1970, the same year as *Caged Bird*. Greer, a controversial debater of women's issues, contested the views of television's prime intellectual, William F. Buckley, American novelist Norman Mailer, and other stouthearted challengers. Angelou claims that she had no prior knowledge of Du Feu's prior marriage to Greer (Crane 1989, 177). He evidently was the author of a book, *Let's Hear It for the Long-Legged Women*, a tanatalizing title that was unretrievable in a search of the Internet at Amazon.com. He had also done a centerfold, almost nude, for the English edition of *Cosmopolitan*, in which his body was sprayed in gold. According to Stephanie Caruana, Du Feu was "the English equivalent of Burt Reynolds" (1989, 30).

When asked about this amazing husband, Angelou painted him in a more professional light: "I was married to a builder, and he told me and told me that building had nothing to do with strength, physical strength. Nor did it have anything to do with sexuality. Instead, it was a matter of being able to look past a wall to the other side" ("Icon" 1997). He also urged Angelou to tell the truth as a writer and not to let her writings be determined by what her readers would think when, in her second autobiography, *Gather Together in My Name*, she revealed that she had been a prostitute. Paul's advice was to be honest about it, to just "say it."

One of the loveliest segments of *Even the Stars Look Lonesome* is her reminiscence of their marriage. She writes of their life together: "We were a rather eccentric, loving, unusual couple determined to live life with flair and laughter" (1997, 5). But the marriage gradually disintegrated. Looking back at the marriage, Angelou speculates that she and Paul were victims of the houses they bought. In the first house there were so many modern appliances that Paul, an architect, had nothing to fix. In the other, with its view of the Golden Gate Bridge, Maya felt jinxed. Whenever she tried to fry chicken or bake bread, her efforts failed, as if the house hated her. After their separation, Maya moved to North Carolina, where she is living now, in order to avoid the pain of running into her or his "replacement" (*Stars* 1997, 8). In summarizing her relationship with Paul, she told Tricia Crane, "It was a great marriage, though we wore it out, we just used it up" (1989, 178).

Angelou in no way abandoned her affections for men after she and Du Feu were divorced in 1980. She told a reporter: "I really enjoy men," then added, "I really enjoy women, too, but not sexually" (Crockett 1997, E1, 8). One of the short essays in *Even the Stars Look Lonesome* is "A Song to Sensuality," in which she describes her love for color, sound, and taste: "I want the crunch of hazelnuts between my teeth and ice cream melting on my tongue" (38). Angelou keeps her senses alive, open to sexual experiences but not dependent on them. As her autobiographies and personal essays reveal, she does not permit any of her sexual relationships to dominate her being.

THE WORK SCHEDULE

During the early days of her first marriage to Tosh Angelos, Maya wanted nothing more than to cook and keep house. Her floors were shiny, her meals "well balanced," her life a tribute to *Good Housekeeping*, a popular magazine for housewives (*Singin' and Swingin'* 26). This attitude did not prevail, nor did the marriage. And when she began seriously to write, she set up a work schedule as rigorous as any housewife's list of daily chores.

Angelou's schedule is described in a number of interviews. Carol Sarler (1989) reports that Angelou gets up at five in the morning and drives to a hotel room, where the staff has been instructed to remove any pictures from the walls. "There's me, the Bible, *Roget's Thesaurus* and some good, dry sherry and I'm at work by 6:30." Angelou writes on legal pads while lying on the bed. She leaves at 12:30, her writing session complete. In the evening she edits what she has written that day, so that ten or twelve pages are whittled down to three or four. During these writing stretches she sees no one, getting her amusement from playing solitaire (1989, 216–17).

Given this routine, one might surmise that a good deal of Angelou's success during the years since Accra is based on her need for self-determination, to control her work schedule, and to allocate sufficient time and energy for any given project. Her writing ritual, one that she has used for years, indicates a firmness of purpose and an inflexible use of time. It seems unlikely to lend itself to deviation in favor of someone else's whim, male or female.

Nor should Angelou's writing routine be viewed as some dreadful ordeal that must be over by lunchtime. It is rather a part of the process of living, a time to focus on the adventures of her life and give them form, make them into art: "Life is pure adventure, and the sooner we realize that, the quicker we will be able to treat life as art" (*Wouldn't Take Nothing for My Journey Now* 66).

EDUCATION

In Stamps, Arkansas, with Mrs. Flowers and on her own, Maya developed a love for the works of Charles Dickens, William Shakespeare, Edgar Allan Poe, and James Weldon Johnson. At the same time, she was also reading black women writers such as Frances Harper, Georgia Douglas Johnson, Anne Spencer, and Jessie Fauset ("Icon" 1997). These writers served as role models and inspirations on Angelou's path toward self-enlightenment (see Chapter 2).

A well-read individual even as a child, thoroughly committed to words and ideas as a young woman, Marguerite Annie Johnson was graduated with honors in the eighth grade from the Lafayette County Training School in Stamps. Soon after, in 1941, the thirteen-year-old

Maya and her brother left the familiarity of their grandmother's store for their mother's boardinghouse in San Francisco, where Vivian Baxter lived with her new husband, Daddy Clidell. She attended George Washington High School where she was befriended by Miss Kirwin, a teacher who, like Mrs. Flowers from Stamps, took a special interest in Maya's education. She also received a scholarship to study dance and theater at the California Labor (Mission) School. She graduated from George Washington High School in 1945, at the end of the Second World War and more than eight months into her pregnancy with Guy.

The autobiographies, especially *Caged Bird* and *Gather Together*, are very much concerned with what Maya knew and how she learned it. As the reader is quick to discover, her most intense learning resulted from personal relationships, family, travel, and growing up as a black woman in white America. Like many of the great African American writers of this century—Claude McKay, Langston Hughes, and James Baldwin— Angelou had not earned a college degree. Instead, her advanced education was achieved through what she described as the "direct instruction" of African American cultural forms: "If you've grown up in an environment where the lore is passed on by insinuation, direct instruction, music, dance, and all other forms of instruction, then . . . that is still the thing out of which you have to move" ("Icon" 1997).

It is part of her genius that she was virtually self-taught, although she did some work in groups where self-criticism was an essential form of the learning process. Prestigious institutions have granted her Honorary Doctorates. In 1975, Smith College and Mills College conferred on Angelou her first two honorary degrees; reportedly she now holds more than fifty. Many people call her Dr. Angelou, a distinction with which she seems comfortable.

FURTHER ACHIEVEMENTS

When *All God's Children Need Traveling Shoes* was published in 1986, Angelou was fifty-eight years of age. By then her life was already rich in achievements of a personal, political, and artistic nature, enough to make one breathless. This section provides a representative list of Angelou's accomplishments in a number of art forms—poetry; children's books; musings; writing for theater, television, and film; directing; acting; and oral presentation.

Poetry

Many readers of Angelou's writings identify her as poet first, an autobiographer second. Since *Maya Angelou: A Critical Companion* focuses on her autobiographies, there are only a few references to her poetic side. Readers are encouraged to study her poems, many of which are included in *The Collected Works of Maya Angelou* (1994).

The dual nature of Angelou's talent is underscored by the fact that within a year of each other, her work received two major nominations, one for her first autobiography and another for her first book of poetry. In 1970, *I Know Why the Caged Bird Sings* received the National Book Award nomination; in 1971, *Just Give Me a Cool Drink of Water 'Fore I Diiie* was nominated for the Pulitzer Prize. She could have achieved a distinguished writing career pursuing either one of these genres. Astonishingly, she did both, so that in the prolific 1970s a new book of poetry emerged shortly before or after a new autobiography.

Many critics think that Angelou's ultimate greatness will be attributed to her poem "On the Pulse of Morning," which she read at the inauguration of William Clinton on January 20, 1993. It was not only the poem itself; it was the vitality of her performance, as she used skills gleaned from years of acting and speaking to arouse the nation.

Before Angelou, only one other American poet, Robert Frost, read an inauguration poem, at the swearing in of John F. Kennedy in 1961. She was the first black, the first woman. When Maya Angelou read "On the Pulse of Morning," she bathed in the magic then surrounding the new administration. The poem, like the incoming president, offered the dream of hope—for Native Americans, gays, homeless, Eskimos, Jews, West Africans, Muslims. It is a long poem, over one hundred lines. It was televised on satellite and delivered electronically around the world.

Her theatrical rendering of "On the Pulse of Morning" is, in a sense, a return to African American oral tradition, when slaves like Frederick Douglass stood on platforms in abolitionist meeting halls to register their concerns about the slave system. The ode also echoes the rhetorical grace of the African American sermon, as practiced and modified by Martin Luther King Jr., Malcolm X, Jesse Jackson, Louis Farrakhan.

"On the Pulse of Morning" is a poem rich with contemporary references to toxic waste and pollution that were the subjects of the 1992 United Nations Conference on Environment and Development. Refer-

ences to mastodons and dinosaurs suggest the prehistoric beasts of
Steven Spielberg's 1993 film, *Jurassic Park*. In these and other instances
Angelou writes with passion about contemporary concerns.

The ode is also influenced, as are the autobiographies, by numerous
African American poets through the oral tradition of spirituals like "Roll,
Jordan, Roll" and the written poetry of James Weldon Johnson, Langston
Hughes, Jean Toomer, and others. In addition, "On the Pulse of Morning" contains echoes of modern African poets and folk artists such as
Kwesi Brew and Efua Sutherland, artists who helped Angelou make contact with African religious beliefs and contemporary African poetry. Finally, "On the Pulse of Morning" is an autobiographical poem, one that
emerges from her conflicts as an American; her experiences as a traveler;
her achievements in public speaking and acting; and her wisdom,
gleaned from years of self-exploration.

In addition to her 1993 inaugural ode, Angelou has further demonstrated her strength as a poet/performer with mass audiences. In the
poem "A Brave and Startling Truth," read in September 1995 in San
Francisco at the 50th anniversary of the United Nations, Angelou spoke
in the same somber tones that were heard at the Clinton inauguration.
Many of the images are similar: the call for peace; the numerous references to the people and places of the world; her insistence on the fragile
nature of what humans have created. It is a majestic, yet sad poem.

For her appearance in November 1995 at the Million Man March in
Washington she recited a poem quite different in tone from the other
two. It is fairly boisterous, a frequently rhymed account of the hardships
of black people which calls for the clapping of hands, the cleansing of
souls. The poem from the Million Man March is written from the point
of view of a black woman inside the struggle but at the same time distanced, advising her marching brothers that they cannot achieve whole-
ness of being until they rise together out of slavery.

Each of these commemorative poems befits a poet laureate—one who
is singled out for a significant achievement or especially in the arts or
sciences. In England, poet laureates are designated by royalty to write
verse on grand occasions, as did both William Wordsworth and Alfred
Lord Tennyson during the nineteenth century. In some American juris-
dictions, in the state of Maryland, for example, African American poet
Lucille Clifton was honored as a poet laureate. Clifton is the author of
many compassionate poems, including "Miss Rosie," a blues tribute to
a haggard "wet brown bag of a woman" who had once been the prize
of Georgia. Angelou cites "Miss Rosie" in *Even the Stars Look Lonesome*,

feeling that the poem explains how the poor and lonely are still able to stand up and reach for a higher place in society.

The United States has had a poet laureate since 1986, when Robert Penn Warren was the first to be bestowed with that honor. The position is attached to that of the poetry consultant to the Library of Congress, with the poet laureate a spokesperson for the arts who is required to give at least one public reading a year. Angelou, so closely connected to the African American tradition represented by Lucille Clifton and by former American laureate Rita Dove, is still exploring her own desire to create meaningful art, what she calls "art for the sake of the soul" (*Stars* 119). Perhaps with the increasing coverage of Angelou's art on television and on the Internet, she will someday be proclaimed an Icon, the people's choice for poet laureate.

Musings

In a 1986 essay, "My Grandson, Home at Last," published in the popular magazine, *Woman's Day*, Angelou traced the efforts to rescue Guy's son, Colin, who had been kidnapped by Guy's estranged wife. The story, written from his grandmother's perspective, describes Guy's pain as a parent and reminds the reader of Maya's own anxiety as she tried to recover Guy from his own kidnapping by Big Mary Dalton related in the powerful sequence of mother-loss in *Gather Together in My Name*.

The delicate personal essay in *Woman's Day* seems to be the antecedent of two books of prose reflections, what Angelou's publisher labels on the dust jacket of *Even the Stars Look Lonesome* a "wise book." A wise book, a collection of informal essays, a series of musings, observations, meditations, or reflections, often interspersed with poetry—each term aptly describes the unconfined genre Angelou has selected for her post-autobiographical writings.

The first of the two, *Wouldn't Take Nothing for My Journey Now* (1993), is dedicated to Oprah Winfrey. The title is from a Negro spiritual, part of which Angelou sang during the "Icon" interview. "It's such a great song, you know. It's a song from slavery. It's got the most amazing kind of spirit." Then, without a pause, Angelou started to sing: "I'm on my journey now / Mt. Zion . . . And I wouldn't take nothin' . . . For my journey now."

Although the title suggests that the book will develop the theme of the journey that dominates her autobiographies, the journeys that occur between its pages are more contemplative than narrative, reminiscent of traditional Asian poetry or of the kind of short meditations dating back to the *Analects* of the Chinese philosopher, Confucius (551–479 B.C.). Whereas the Confucian reflections were told by a male to males, Angelou alters the traditional gender expectations in both books of musings, rendering her advice from a woman's perspective.

Wouldn't Take Nothing for My Journey Now is a tiny book, consisting of a mere 139 pages. Nonetheless, Angelou manages to say a lot within the scope of the text, on topics that range from instructions on how to be creative with fabrics to profound issues dealing with death, racism, Christianity, and West African religious beliefs. There are also solid representations of Angelou's quoted sayings, including the well-known statement: "Human beings are more alike than unalike" (11).

The book is at its best when it is autobiographical—when it recounts episodes involving Maya's brother or son or mother or grandmother, or when it presents a separate episode consistent with the Maya character of the autobiographies. The section, "New Directions," for instance, further relates the heroic story from *I Know Why the Caged Bird Sings* about how Annie Henderson saved her family during the Great Depression by selling homemade meat pies to area factory workers. Other segments involving Annie Henderson include a fantasy in which Maya sees her grandmother standing "thousands of feet up in the air on nothing visible" (74). This exaggerated description of Annie's physical and spiritual power is reminiscent of similar scenes in *Caged Bird*, although the mystery of Annie's faith seems less convincing here because it is treated briefly and outside the broader autobiographical framework.

In a comparable sketch, Angelou creates an engaging portrait of her Aunt Tee from Los Angeles, an old woman who had spent almost sixty years working for white families and observing the sadness of their lives. As her employers began to age and not longer need her services, Aunt Tee started to throw parties every Saturday night, with fried chicken, dancing, and card playing. One night she discovers her elderly employers peeking in at the party, begging to be allowed to just sit and watch.

The story is effective, although Angelou uses it not as a narrative in itself, but as a springboard to reflect on life and art and money and power, a typical technique in constructing an essay. This kind of sketch, interesting as it might be, demands the structural cohesion of the longer, autobiographical work to make it part of a larger pattern and not a mere snippet. It would be nicely contained, for example, in a sixth autobiography.

Of the various autobiographical moments in *Wouldn't Take Nothing for My Journey Now*, the one that seems to sustain itself most effectively is "Extending the Boundaries." The seven-page story is sufficiently developed to convey a narrative sense; it also gives us a Maya with the three-dimensional sophistication of character that we find in *The Heart of a Woman* and *All God's Children Need Traveling Shoes*. She is a woman admired for her achievements but pitied for her inappropriate behavior and faulty conclusions.

In "Extending the Boundaries," she describes being honored in the late 1960s at Terry's Pub, a bar for "the black and hip in New York City" (107), after having been named the *New York Post*'s Person of the Week. The regulars toast and cheer her, then eventually go back to their accustomed patterns. Having drunk at least five martinis and desperately in search of a partner, she interrupts a group of African American journalists and begins a litany of her skills in housekeeping, cooking, languages, and lovemaking. She demands to know why, with all of those qualities, she isn't acceptable to them. In a painful moment of self-awareness, Angelou realizes that she had "overstepped the written rules which I knew I should have respected. Instead, I had brazenly and boldly come to their table and spoken out on, of all things, loneliness" (111). She starts to cry.

Later she is escorted home by a sympathetic but critical male friend, who leaves her at the door. After she sobers up, she begins to reflect on her marriage to Tosh Angelos and her sexuality in general. Because the marriage to Tosh had failed, she has been determined not to look for love except among African Americans. Her experience with the black men in the bar, though, had somehow changed her opinion. If a man came along, whatever his race, she would "not struggle too hard," as long as he was sincere and could make her laugh (113).

This mini-episode, seemingly detached from the autobiographies, is nonetheless related to them by way of her needs, her aggressiveness, her lack of control. Similar in tone to the embarrassing quarrel with her husband's mistress in *The Heart of a Woman*, "Exceeding the Boundaries" reveals a narrator more distraught and misguided than would be expected in a more conventional self-portrait. The pervading autobiographical content saves *Wouldn't Take Nothing for My Journey Now* from its tendency to sermonize on proper conduct or virtue, as in the sermon on death ("Death and the Legacy") or the several paragraphs on the morality of planting and cultivation ("At Harvestime").

Even the Stars Look Lonesome was published in 1997, four years after *Journey*. It is similar in tone and layout, although the text is six pages longer. At the time of our interview, Angelou was proofing the final copy, and confidently anticipating the release of *Stars*: "I think its the best writing I've ever done" ("Icon" 1997).

The book of reflections candidly discusses her mother Vivian Baxter, her husband Vusumsi Make, her son Guy, and other people prominent in the autobiographies. It also contains excellent discussions about African history, West African art, and aging.

Two of the most enjoyable essays were, first, "Art for the Sake of the Soul," which begins with Lucille Clifton's "Miss Rosie" and recollects, among other things, an impromptu concert in Morocco that occurred during the original *Porgy and Bess* tour in the mid-1950s. A dancer and not a singer, Angelou was called on to perform. Unable to offer an operatic rendition, she sang Momma Henderson's favorite spiritual, "I'm a poor pilgrim of sorrow," to the shouting and clapping of the almost five thousand people in the audience. The essay moves from her autobiographical experience to a statement on the universality of art, ending with a strong plea for governmental funding of projects in the arts and in the theater, a position that Angelou has held for quite some time.

In a provocative 1955 interview with Ken Kelley of *Mother Jones* magazine, she spoke out against conservatives in the government who want to stop funding for the arts: "The conservative right has decided that artists are apart from the people. That's *ridiculous!* I mean, at our best the writer, painter, architect, actor, dancer, folk singer—we *are* the people." She advises artists to sing, dance, and perform in public places so that the young do not have to surrender their dreams. (Available from http://www.mojones.com/mother_jones/MJ95/kelley.htmlrnet; Internet.)

The other recollection in *Stars* that has tremendous vitality is "Rural Museums—Southern Romance." Also concerned with art and the preservation of culture, "Rural Museums" is a grim recounting of Angelou's journey to a slave museum in Louisiana, not far from Baton Rouge. The artifacts included a depressing statue of a bent figure, "Uncle Jack," the exemplary Negro slave; an overseer's house; a slave collar; nineteenth-century carriages being buffed by an African American male; and some still-standing slave cabins, very neatly furnished. In Angelou's view, the museum captured in its orderly presentations "the romance of slavery," eliminating any real sense of the brutality, the beatings, the cramped hovels, the exhaustion, the hunger. Missing from the reconstructed scene was "our historical truth" (94, 95), truth being just what a museum should uphold.

Although both of these wise books make use of the travel motif, that theme is more central to *Even the Stars Look Lonesome* than to its earlier, journey-titled companion piece. Angelou gives the reader some priceless glimpses of her self in each of the collections, although the frequent citations of poetry seem out of proportion if what the reader anticipates is an updated array of insights from the woman whose autobiographies have set the standard for length, breadth, and historical relevance.

In assessing Angelou's two books of reflections, one must be cautious in not confusing genres. The reader should be continually aware that both *Journey* and *Stars* contain a great deal of quoted secondary material. Above all, the reader should know that they are not autobiographies. Journalist Sandra Crockett, in a September 1997, feature article in the *Baltimore Sun*, identifies *Even the Stars Look Lonesome* as part of Angelou's "continuing series of autobiographical books" (E1, 8). Although both texts clearly have autobiographical moments, they are in no way a continuation of the solid, book-length journeys into the self that Angelou has been conducting since the 1970 appearance of *I Know Why the Caged Bird Sings*. Neither *Journey* nor *Stars*, collections of short, informal essays, should be mistaken for autobiography, the genre that forms the basis of this work, *Maya Angelou: A Critical Companion*.

Children's Books

Angelou's children's books belong outside this survey, with the exception of *Life Doesn't Frighten Me* (1993), an illustrated version of a poem from her most popular volume, *And Still I Rise* (1978). *Life Doesn't Frighten Me* was done in collaboration with artist Jean-Michel Basquiat (1960–1988). Its fear of the outside world is related thematically to Maya's fear of crosses and white invaders, eloquently depicted in her autobiography, *I Know Why the Caged Bird Sings*. The short text offers a series of negative images—barking dogs, ghosts, and so forth—all softened with the repeated line: "Life doesn't frighten me at all." Thus Angelou relegates fear to the dream world.

Her message is an effort to combat the dreadful reality she experienced as a black child in Alabama. It also speaks to the fears of many of today's African American children: the AIDS threat; guns in the schools; gratuitous rape of the kind that Maya herself endured as a child. The poetic images are brilliantly complemented by Basquiat's illustrations of masked stick figures and black-faced grizzlies, testaments to urban vio-

...at predict his own early death. Basquiat, friend of Andy Warhol
...other famed New York artists, died at the age of 27 of an overdose
...heroin-cocaine.

Theater and Television Work

After Angelou decided to return from Ghana to the United States in
the mid-sixties, she immersed herself in a different America, where
blackness was a matter of pride, where a creative racial identity was
emerging in the cities. In 1966, she finished a short play, *The Least of
These*, which was staged in Los Angeles. In 1968, at the age of forty, she
wrote a ten-part series on African influences, *Black, Blues, Black*, which
was aired on educational television, followed by an impressive array of
achievements in television and on screen. In 1972, she wrote both the
screenplay and the music for the television special, *Georgia, Georgia*,
about two African American women visiting Switzerland, thus becoming
"the first Black woman to have a screenplay produced" (*Current Biography* 1994, 28). Four years later, her play, *And Still I Rise*, was performed
in California, and she wrote two specials for television, "The Legacy"
and "The Inheritors." These television triumphs were followed, in 1977,
by a prize-winning documentary television series on African Americans
and the arts. In 1982, she wrote another television screenplay, *Sister, Sister* and in 1985, a play, *The Southern Journey*. Angelou also did the screenplay and the music for the popular film version of *I Know Why the Caged
Bird Sings*, directed by Fielder Cook. The video, which is currently available, benefits from a comparison/contrast with the book, especially in
terms of what the film omits, since the film ends at the eighth grade
graduation, thus avoiding her troubled adolescence.

Angelou's professional career onstage was probably initiated in 1957,
when she performed in *Calypso Heatwave*, an off-Broadway production.
In 1960 she and Godfrey Cambridge wrote, directed, and performed in
Cabaret for Freedom, a fund-raiser for Martin Luther King Jr. She was also
the premier dancer for the touring production of *Porgy and Bess*, a role
that demanded performing as well as dancing skills. Her great stage role,
though, was in 1961, as the White Queen in Jean Genet's award-winning
play *The Blacks*. Her participation in both the original off-Broadway play
and in its European revival is described in *The Heart of a Woman* and in
All God's Children Need Traveling Shoes. In 1966, after she had returned
from Ghana, she acted in a modern version of *Medea*, as the Greek

woman who murdered her children. In 1973, at the age of forty-five, she was nominated for a Tony for her performance as Mary Todd Lincoln's dressmaker in the Broadway production, *Look Away*.

Angelou also had many acting triumphs in television and film, one being her Tony nomination, in 1977, for portraying Kunta Kinte's grandmother in Alex Haley's explosive miniseries, *Roots*. In 1982, when she was fifty-four, she performed the narration for *Humanities Through the Arts*, a series sponsored by public television. In 1995, she appeared in John Singleton's movie *Poetic Justice* and in Jocelyn Moorhouse's film, *How to Make an American Quilt*.

During her career, Angelou has also had some experiences directing for stage, television, and film. In 1974 she directed a film, *All Day Long*, from her original screenplay, while in 1968 she directed a play, *Moon on a Rainbow Shawl*, written by Errol John. But it was not until 1997 that she engaged in her first major project as a director, with the film *Down on the Delta*, starring Wesley Snipes and her *How to Make an American Quilt* costar Alfre Woodard. The film is about a couple from Mississippi who head for Chicago looking for a better life.

Special Awards

In addition to being a recognized actor and writer, Angelou has also received a number of special awards that commemorate her service to the humanities. The list is partial, given the wide range of tributes Angelou has received from civic groups across the country. Many of the works of art in her sculpture garden, for instance, testify to her being honored by institutions who do not always boast international reputations.

One of her most prestigious awards occurred in 1975, when President Gerald Ford named her to the American Revolution Bicentennial Council. Angelou wore this hat gracefully, as a patriotic duty: "I am an American, as much as the Irish who live here are Americans. . . . There are many things I'm proud of and many things I'm disappointed in, referring to my country. It would be the same if I lived in Birmingham, Alabama, or Birmingham, England. But I am an American" ("Icon" 1997).

In 1976, a year after the appointment from President Ford, the *Ladies' Home Journal* named Maya Angelou Woman of the Year in Communications. In 1977, President Jimmy Carter named her to a commission in observance of International Women's Year.

She has also been honored by foundations, receiving a Yale University Fellowship in 1970 and the enviable Rockefeller Foundation Scholarship in 1975. In 1982, at the age of fifty-four, she was named Reynolds Professor of American Studies at Wake Forest University in Winston-Salem, North Carolina. Two years later, the new governor, James B. Hunt, appointed her to the board of the North Carolina Arts Council.

Meanwhile, her work continues to diversify. In the past several years, Angelou has reportedly communicated to her public through the Prodigy Internet service provider, and has organized churches on Public Television. She has also participated in the Black Image circuit—African American women models, lawyers, and writers tour designated cities conducting workshops offering tips on clothes, poise, cosmetics, and problem solving. Women who have attended these workshops say that Angelou's participation in workshops with black middle-class women should not be trivialized, for through her example, she is offering black women an opportunity to direct their talents toward achievable goals.

Her service to major institutions as well as her remarkable self-confidence as a speaker have opened other doors for Maya Angelou, especially in the area of public policy. She wears the cloak of wise woman and stateswoman—sometimes on daytime television with her close friend Oprah Winfrey; sometimes for organizations such as the Women's Foundation, which sold well over two thousand tickets when she spoke in San Francisco during the spring of 1997; and more often in college lecture halls, where seating is sold out long before the actual event.

Keeping up with a woman as vibrant as Maya Angelou takes a team of researchers working around the clock. Fortunately, Sharon E. Snow, Curator of Rare Books at the Z. Smith Reynolds Library at Wake Forest University, has already made progress in providing access to Angelou's letters and manuscripts, as well as the mountain of writings and video clips bearing her name. The archives offer hundreds of reviews; the typed manuscript of Angelou's play, *Sister, Sister*; a letter from Malcolm X to Maya Angelou, dated January 15, 1965; speeches delivered on college campuses; and other material voluminous enough to occupy 100 linear feet of library shelving. When told that there is a significant body of scholarship about her work available in school libraries and asked, "Could you give me any special message to them as they read the autobiographies and the criticism?" she replied, "Somebody needs to tell young people, listen, I did this and I did that. You may encounter many defeats, but you must not be defeated" ("Icon" 1997). These familiar words of encouragement are especially applicable to an examination of the autobiographical genre and Maya Angelou's place within African American and American autobiographical tradition.

The Genre of Autobiography

AUTOBIOGRAPHY AND GENRE

The French word genre means a classification of literary works according to type—lyric, narrative, dramatic—which are further divided into novel, short story, epic poem, tragedy, and so forth. According to Meyer H. Abrams, genre is of use to the reader because it "creates a set of expectations which . . . enable the reader to make the work intelligible" (1993, 77). In other words, if the reader knows for a fact that Angelou's *I Know Why the Caged Bird Sings* is an autobiography, then the reader also expects the sequel, *Gather Together in My Name*, to have understandable characteristics of the genre, such as first-person narration, a chronological order, and an emphasis on the self.

Autobiography is a major literary genre, the form that Maya Angelou uses in her long prose works. Broken down, the word auto/bio/graphy means self/life/story, the narrative of the events in a person's life. It is also known as life writing or the literature of self-revelation. According to Alfred Kazin, autobiography "uses fact as a strategy [It is a] history of a self, [and exhibits a] concern for the self as a character" (1964, 213).

A number of critics have classified Angelou's five volumes as autobiographical fiction and not as autobiographies, for the apparent reason that Angelou amplifies the autobiographical tone by using dialogue—by having another character or characters speak to the narrator. According

to Eugenia Collier, the writing techniques Angelou uses in her autobiographies are the same as the devices used in writing fiction: vividly
conceived characters and careful development of theme, setting, plot,
and language (1986).

At first glance, it is useful to view *Caged Bird* as a *Bildungsroman*, a
German word that means a "novel of education" or a "coming-of-age"
story. Because *Caged Bird* begins in childhood and ends in young adult-
hood, with Maya giving birth to a baby boy, *Caged Bird* has been considered a *Bildungsroman*. Looking at the British *Bildungsroman, Mill on the
Floss* (1860), there are many similarities between George Eliot's novel and
Maya Angelou's first autobiography. Both are about the coming-of-age
of strong-willed young women; both focus on the heroine's close relationship to her brother; both examine the effects of literature on character; both center strongly around family and community life. But while
Mill on the Floss is a developed work of fiction, a story that ends, according to Eliot's deliberate plan, with her heroine's death in a flood,
Angelou's autobiography is an unfinished narrative, told in the first person by the adult who recollects it years later. Angelou insists on calling
her works autobiographies, not novels. For her, autobiography is a special form, consciously chosen as her most effective genre. In an interview,
she told Jackie Kay that "I think I am the only serious writer who has
chosen the autobiographical form as the main form to carry my work,
my expression" (1989, 195).

Most readers of autobiographies have clear expectations about the
characteristics of the genre. First, it should be written rather than spoken.
Second, it must have a first-person narrator. Third, it should be of man-
ageable length, one or two volumes. Fourth, it should be arranged chron-
ologically, in an order that roughly corresponds to the significant events
of the narrator's life.

Exceptions to these standards are of course numerous; one of the most
extreme is Gertrude Stein's *The Autobiography of Alice B. Toklas* (1933).
Although autobiographies are typically written from the first-person
point of view, Stein pretends to use the first-person perspective of her
friend, the Alice B. Toklas of the title. Stein's autobiography thus approaches fiction in its playful invention of a first-person narrator who is
actually a third person. James Weldon Johnson, a favorite writer of Angelou's and an autobiographer in his own right, wrote a unique book
that combined the perspectives of both the novel and the autobiography.
He called it *The Autobiography of an Ex-Colored Man* (1912), and in the
first printing it had an anonymous author, which made readers puzzle

about the author's race. Johnson's point of view in this now-famous book was as inventive in its way as Gertrude Stein's was in *The Autobiography of Alice B. Toklas*. Like Stein's contrived Alice, so Johnson's narrator is not actually James Weldon Johnson but a pretend white man, the fictionalized self-portrait of a light-skinned black who passes as white in order to be esteemed and rewarded by others.

The popular Lakota Sioux narrative, *Black Elk Speaks*, is also an exception to the standard autobiography, not in its structure but in its presentation. The very title, *Black Elk Speaks*, indicates an oral or spoken autobiography, told by Black Elk over the course of many years, but put into writing by a European transcriber, John G. Neihardt. In his effort to shape Black Elk's story into an artistic whole, Neihardt writes parts of the beginning and final chapters, thus defining the narrator's identity. This superlative collaboration between Black Elk and his transcriber resulted in the "first Indian autobiography" (Holly 1979, 121).

One critic of the genre, William L. Howarth (1980), has isolated certain elements common to all standard autobiographies. First is "character," which designates the narrator, the one who tells the story and acts within it, as opposed to the more distanced "author." The second element, "technique," includes stylistic concerns such as metaphors, structure, verb tense. Howarth's third element is "theme," which addresses not only personal issues like love and death, but also political, cultural, and historical matters affecting the autobiographer, in Angelou's case, the Great Depression of the early 1930s, the civil-rights movement in America in the 1960s and the liberation movements in Africa in the same decade.

Additionally, autobiographical theme is affected by literary tradition. If a writer reads or thinks about a favorite book, he/she is likely to echo its structure or its ideas, either knowingly or unknowingly. The writer is thus "influenced." A literary influence occurs when a piece of literature or a specific creative form, existing in the near or distant past, affects the language, metaphors, style, structure, and/or philosophy of any given work. To determine the influence of poet Georgia Douglas Johnson on Angelou's *The Heart of a Woman*, for instance, one needs some knowledge of genres, of titles, of dates of composition, of mutual metaphors, of existing attitudes towards black women, and so on.

Angelou is quite open about her literary influences, naming at least a dozen in *Caged Bird*. Authors and genres are therefore likely to have influenced her autobiographies. Christine Froula (1986) makes the connection between Maya's rape and Shakespeare's two thousand–line poem

"The Rape of Lucrece," which Maya memorizes on regaining speech. Other influences include authors such as William Shakespeare and Edgar Allan Poe; and genres such as slave narratives, spirituals, poetry, and serial autobiographies, as well as individual autobiographies in the African American tradition. See Chapter 7 for an alternative reading of signifying and the black tradition in Angelou's fifth autobiography, *All God's Children Need Traveling Shoes*.

Other than their length and thematic material, Angelou's autobiographies conform to the standard structure of the autobiography: they are written, they are single-authored, and they are chronological. As will be observed in forthcoming chapters, they contain Howarth's required elements of character, technique, and theme. However, the five volumes that make up Angelou's series far exceed the standard number of volumes in an autobiography, so much so that they are in a sub-genre known as "serial autobiographies."

SERIAL AUTOBIOGRAPHIES

A serial autobiography is a set of two or more related texts that reflect on, predict, and echo each other, so that they are seen as parts of a whole. For later volumes there are earlier ones behind them that must be recollected, just as in the larger tradition there are authors from the past— Frederick Douglass, Zora Neale Hurston, Paul Laurence Dunbar—who must be remembered if the reader is to maximize his/her experience. Some African American critics call this attention to past literary tradition by the name of "signifying."

Angelou has written five autobiographies and is considering a sixth volume. She enjoys the multiple form, the "stretching" required in going from book to book: "I pray that in each book I am getting closer to finding the mystery of really manipulating and being manipulated by this medium, to pulling it open, stretching it" (qtd. in Kay 1989, 195). While the continuous fluctuation of the serial form allows the writer a freedom not available in the fixed, single autobiography, it also has pitfalls, including the increased need for transitions, for cross-references, for continuity, for discipline.

There are numerous examples of the multiple autobiography within the black literary tradition. The foremost would be Frederick Douglass's two-part autobiography: the 1845 *Narrative of the Life of Frederick Douglass*, followed by a second autobiography, *My Bondage and My Freedom* in

1855. The first volume is so widely considered to be the model slave narrative that few contemporary readers have become familiar with its sequel, *My Bondage and My Freedom*, a broader and more detailed work than its predecessor. William L. Andrews calls it that "rare 'I-narrative' of the American 1850s," one that explores Douglass's "identity, mission, and message" (1986, xxvi).

Richard Wright, well-known for the best-selling novel *Native Son* (1940), is also the author of a passionate autobiography, *Black Boy* (1945), a recollection of childhood and adolescence, frequently compared to *I Know Why the Caged Bird Sings*. In 1977, some time after Wright's death in 1960, a sequel to *Black Boy* was discovered, thus changing its status from single to serial autobiography. The sequel, *American Hunger*, written in 1944 at the time he was working on *Black Boy*, is a political autobiography that covers Wright's early involvement with the Communist Party in Chicago and New York. The volumes are ages apart in tone and narrative style: *American Hunger* is dry and abstract in comparison with the painful and compelling *Black Boy*. Reading the two works as a pair makes the reader recognize just how smooth Angelou's transitions are from volume to volume, how consistent her character.

These are but a few of the important serial autobiographies published by African Americans since the Civil War. White authors who have extended the initial autobiographical impulse into a series include Sherwood Anderson, Gertrude Stein, Anais Nin, and Theodore Dreiser. One of the twentieth century's most admired novelists, Doris Lessing, has been working for several years on a three-part serial autobiography. The first, *Under My Skin* (1994), begins with her childhood on a farm in Zimbabwe in southern Africa, while the second, *Walking in the Shade* (1997), chronicles her life as a writer and single mother. Her affinities with Angelou are many.

The serial autobiographer who has the most in common with Angelou is the white American playwright, Lillian Hellman. Almost as prolific as Angelou, Hellman wrote a serial autobiography consisting of four volumes: *An Unfinished Woman* (1970); *Pentimento* (1973); *Scoundrel Time* (1976); and *Maybe* (1980). The first of the series, *An Unfinished Woman*, won the 1970 National Book Award for best book in Arts and Letters— the very same year that Angelou was nominated for (but did not receive) the same award for *I Know Why the Caged Bird Sings*.

Hellman and Angelou have much in common. Both women developed their sense of language and dialogue by working in the theater, with Hellman receiving praise for her early play, *The Children's Hour* (1934), a frightening drama about a schoolgirl's destructive behavior toward two women teachers. After her return from Ghana, Angelou was active in the theater in terms of writing, acting, and directing, although she never achieved Hellman's stature as a playwright. Both Hellman and Angelou positioned their autobiographies in America and continental Europe, with Angelou taking her international setting farther, into Africa. Both writers have been publically lauded in their lifetimes. Lillian Hellman received a standing ovation at the 1977 Academy Awards for the film *Julia*, which was based on an episode from her autobiography, *Pentimento*, while Angelou has had many similar honors, her greatest being the invitation to read "On the Pulse of Morning" at the 1993 inauguration of President Clinton.

Given these resemblances, it is a bit surprising to read the concluding interview in Dolly A. McPherson's *Order Out of Chaos* (1990), only to discover a strong rivalry between Angelou and Hellman. Angelou's resentment of Hellman is supposedly based on literary distinctions. Angelou tells McPherson that Hellman's books are "one-dimensional" or "romantic." Her black characters are stiff as "cardboard," while her white ones fail to represent the masses (1990, 135).

AUTOBIOGRAPHY AND TRUTH

In *Design and Truth in Autobiography* (1960), Roy Pascal theorizes that autobiography must be a presentation of truth—truth in characterization, truth in relationship to the world, truth in point of view. Many other critics share Pascal's opinion, including Angelou's biographer, Dolly A. McPherson (1990, 72). Another follower of Pascal insists that autobiographies are "limited by the writer's need to speak in the spirit of the truth." He warns that the autobiographer should "never allow himself to jeopardize credibility" (Mandel 1968, 224).

Angelou's views to some extent diverge from the conventional notion of autobiography as truth. Angelou, who is well aware of the truth-in-autobiography theory, admitted to George Plimpton that she has on occasion "fiddled with" the truth, combining several characters for literary effect or being considerate to people who are still alive (1994, 18). In this author's interview of June 16, 1997, Angelou stated that: "Certain things overstate the facts . . . I want to always leave something for the reader to do, to imagine, to fantasize. I want to tell the truth but I can't because

I'd ruin the thing." When asked what she meant by "ruin the thing," she responded: "Well, losing the reader is ruining the thing. If I tell the truth . . . in language which shocks but does not terrify, which shakes somebody up but doesn't make them run away, I may impart something which might be of help" ("Icon").

What frequently goes unsaid when discussing the so-called truth in the history of African American autobiography is that in many instances the truth has been censored or hidden out of the need for self-protection. Black autobiographers writing during the abolitionist movement (the antislavery movement that flourished during the several decades before the Civil War) had to restrain or disguise their opinions, even toward their compassionate editors. Slave narratives withheld certain ideas that might have put the slave teller in danger, no matter how well intentioned the transcriber might be—secret hopes for rebellion; a buried contempt for white men as rapists; and other hostile opinions toward white benefactors. Jennifer Fleischner, author of *Mastering Slavery* (1996), insists there is much to learn from the gaps or omissions that appear in the slave narratives, since these gaps can reveal disguised attitudes towards self, race, and resistance. The nineteenth-century slave narrator, a recognized victim of slavery, was supposed to give an honest account of life under the plantation system, with its beatings from white overseers and sexual abuses from brutal white owners. What the slave wrote not only had to be "true," but its truth had to be upheld or verified, in the preface or appendix, by conscientious white editors, publishers, and friends. Thus, the *Narrative of the Life of Frederick Douglass* was verified in the preface by abolitionist leaders William Lloyd Garrison and Wendell Phillips.

Although Maya Angelou identifies with slavery and verifies its power in her life and works, her concept of truth and black womanhood is transformed by its contemporary content. In *Caged Bird*, for example, she records a life story begun in fear of crosses burning in the night, a life that is directly affected by the brutal remnants of slavery. Her story ends much like a slave narrative—in celebration of her personal freedom and of black cultural achievements in Africa and America. Angelou's autobiographies, documented with historical personages and events, verify the changing attitudes towards race and gender from 1928 to 1965.

As David Levering Lewis observes, her stories contain such "inner truthfulness that each of her books is a continuing autobiography of much of Afro-America" (1997, 133). Sondra O'Neale alters the truth factor, locating it in a feminist vision. She claims that the specific truth

Angelou tells is the truth about the lives of black women. From this perspective Angelou is able to correct historical errors and offer a role model not often seen in American culture (1984, 35).

As a woman, Angelou tells truths about all women's lives. For black women the neglect of their histories and their literary works has been devastating, although a change occurred in the 1970s and 1980s, when Alice Walker, Toni Morrison, Toni Cade Bambara, Maya Angelou, and so many other black women exploded into bookstores and lecture halls, telling their stories. Angelou addresses her own issues—about rape, marriage, talent, community, responsibility to her son—from the perspective of an African American woman. In so doing she introduces material not very often developed by autobiographers, black or white. As Joanne Braxton notes, Angelou's autobiographical sources derive from "her celebration of the black women who nurtured her" (1989, 197).

Readers intrigued by Angelou's life will learn, from biographical sources, interviews, and Internet sources, an assortment of facts about Angelou, her son Guy, her brother Bailey, or her grandson Colin, who was kidnapped by Guy's former wife. All of this is engrossing material upon which to draw. But for the purist this sort of after-the-fact information is irrelevant; the truth and the integrity of an autobiography must be contained within the text itself.

AUTOBIOGRAPHY AND THE BLACK LITERARY TRADITION

Gender

Maya Angelou is one of the many twentieth-century African American women whose works are written in the form of autobiography. Angelou has much in common with Zora Neale Hurston (1901–1960), whose autobiography, *Dust Tracks on a Road* (1942), tells how she rose above her origins in Eatonvile, an all-black town in Florida, to become a famous folklorist and novelist. Like Hurston in Florida, Angelou in Arkansas flavors her autobiography with the language of black folk culture. As Angelou writes autobiographical texts that include the Bambara people of Africa, Hurston has written books like *Tell My Horse* (1938), which describe her experiences with voodoo ritual in Haiti.

A second woman autobiographer whom Angelou resembles is the poet Gwendolyn Brooks (1917–   ), in that both Brooks and Angelou locate their autobiographical experiences in Africa. In her autobiography *Report from Part One* (1972), Brooks describes her journey to East Africa in 1971. Her arrival is mixed with joy in being in the land of her ancestors but sadness in seeing her own language diminish in importance. Like Angelou, Brooks is unable to resolve the contradictions between being an African American but identifying with Africans, for whom she remains a stranger.

A third autobiography that demands attention in this survey is Anne Moody's *Coming of Age in Mississippi* (1968). A student at Tougaloo, an historically black college in Mississippi, Moody took part in a sit-in at a Woolworth's lunch counter, in what was to become one of the early, memorable actions of the civil-rights movement. Like Angelou, Moody knew and worked with Martin Luther King Jr. As an activist living in Mississippi, however, Moody was far closer to the grass roots movement of the 1960s than was Angelou. Angelou's civil-rights story, told from the perspective of the Northern Coordinator of the Southern Christian Leadership Conference, lacks the immediacy found in Moody's autobiography.

Further books for exploration in the area of the black women's autobiographical tradition are Nikki Giovanni's partial autobiography, *Gemini: An Extended Autobiographical Statement on My First Twenty-Five Years of Being a Black Poet* (1971), which begins well but loses its autobiographical structure, becoming part book review and part essay; and bell hooks's *Bone Black: Memories of Girlhood* (1996), a free-flowing autobiography that attempts to offer black women a model for writing about their lives.

In addition to gender distinctions (and these categories frequently overlap), one needs to place Angelou's work within the historical development of African American autobiography. Two of the major black autobiographical structures, the slave narrative and the travel autobiography, are discussed more fully later in this chapter. Other significant forms are the prison autobiography, the success narrative, and the autobiography of the artist.

The Prison Autobiography

The prison autobiography is the genre most directly related to the earliest black narrative form, the slave narrative; they share many themes, among them captivity, self-education, mistreatment, and the desire to escape. The prison autobiography achieved prominence in the period surrounding the civil-rights movement of the 1960s, through the writings of Eldridge Cleaver, George Jackson, Angela Davis, Malcolm X, and other articulate defenders of the black liberation movement.

Cleaver's *Soul on Ice* (1968) was written from Folsom prison by the man who rose to become a leader of the Black Panther party. Cleaver describes how his prison experience made it possible to free his mind from being oppressed by the white woman, whom he has come to see as an ogre, her claws sunk into his chest. Cleaver's attack on white women had a significant effect in discouraging the interracial sexuality common in the early 1960s. Cleaver used his prison years as a way to deal with his troubled sexuality and to construct an ideology supported by the writings of Karl Marx, Vladimir Ilyich Lenin, and other theorists.

Reading, learning, and being able to recognize historical distortions are part of the mental discipline described in prison literature, for it was only within the walls of the jail that many African American leaders were able to set their minds free. In his autobiography, Malcolm X is frequently thankful for the prison experience, for in jail he taught himself to read: "I don't think anybody ever got more out of going to prison than I did. . . . Where else but in a prison could I have attacked my ignorance by being able to study intensely sometimes as much as fifteen hours a day" (1965, 41).

For Angela Davis, who was arrested by the FBI on conspiracy charges in 1970, her prison autobiography *Angela Davis* (1974) is extremely impersonal, as if she were deliberately avoiding the kinds of sentiment that would identify her as a female. In a philosophical application of the knowledge that she already had when she went to prison, she denounces its disorganized structure and inadequate facilities. Davis notes that the library holds little other than "bad literature whose sole function was to create emotional paths of escape" (51), although she does locate the autobiography of W.E.B. Du Bois. When Davis learns that she is permitted to order books from publishers, she orders ten copies of George Jackson's radical autobiography *Soledad Brother* (1970), which the guards prevent her from distributing. Despite the strict regulations, Davis is able to learn through her prison experience through the relationships she forms with women prisoners. She also relishes visits from friends and lawyers affiliated with the Communist Party.

Angelou's autobiographies share elements of the prison narrative, but on a symbolic rather than an actual level. The central image of the caged bird, presented throughout the five volumes, represents her imprisonment within the racist structure of Stamps, Arkansas, with the Ku Klux

Klan and its unequal educational opportunities. After she is released from Stamps, the racial discrimination continues, but with less intensity. She becomes aware of other forms of imprisonment—through drugs, marriage, the economic system.

The Success Narrative

Many black professionals have written different kinds of autobiographies that may be called first-person success narratives. This genre, meant to offer helpful models for young black men and women, is important to the black tradition because it encourages a positive response from a community where drugs and easy money are often more highly rewarded than hard work. In *Along This Way* (1933), James Weldon Johnson, one of Angelou's major influences as a child, traces his development from birth, when he was nursed by a white mammy in Jacksonville, Florida, to varied successes as lawyer, songwriter, statesman, novelist, lecturer, and occupant of the chair of Creative Literature at Fisk University, an historic black institution.

Many African American success autobiographies have been written not by creative artists but by doctors, scholars, ministers, or other professionals. Dr. Ben Carson, a surgeon at the Johns Hopkins Hospital in Baltimore, Maryland, has influenced many people in the community with his autobiography *Gifted Hands* (1993). In addition to his writings, Carson gives inspirational talks on the need to be a good student and the need to listen to the advice of teachers and family members. Again, it is Carson's race that makes his words so powerful, for his speeches and his book are directed toward uplifting the underpaid and the underprivileged.

Also included in this category is Henry Louis Gates Jr.'s autobiography, *Colored People* (1995). Gates, America's foremost critic of African American literature, describes his coming to age in Piedmont, a small black town in West Virginia. Although there are hardships, he relates closely to his own supportive community and to his family. At the end of the autobiography, Gates has come home for vacation from Yale University—Yale being a symbol of success and superior future performance. Ironically, the autobiography ends at the annual mill picnic, an honored black tradition about to end because of integration. But integration is too late. As the narrator's aunt explains: "By the time those crackers made us join them, she added, we didn't want to go" (211).

Gates's witty and vivid descriptions of the folks in Piedmont, West

Virginia, have a texture similar to Angelou's portrayal of the black community of Stamps, with their rural ways. What biographer Robert E. Hemenway says of Zora Neale Hurston seems sadly true of Gates and Angelou as well. To attain success in an autobiography, the black narrator must see himself or herself as having risen above the associations of class and culture symbolized by the very rural black people who inspired the work (1977, 281).

Angelou's last two autobiographies have strong traces of the success narrative. Her acting career, described in *The Heart of a Woman*, peaked when she portrayed the White Queen in Jean Genet's play, *The Blacks*. Her fund-raising revue, *Cabaret for Freedom*, which she coauthored with actor Godfrey Cambridge, won her the respect of Martin Luther King Jr. and a leadership position in his organization, the Southern Christian Leadership Conference (SCLC). In *All God's Children Need Traveling Shoes*, Angelou was associate editor of the *Arab Observer* and did free-lance writing for the *Ghanaian Times*. She also successfully organized a solidarity demonstration in Ghana in support of Martin Luther King's 1965 march on Washington. These achievements alone could make the claim that Angelou's later autobiographies belong to the category of the success autobiography.

Literary Autobiography

Angelou's writings appear to fall into yet a third category, literary autobiography or, by extension, the autobiography of a writer, artist, dancer, or other art/professional. As a rule, writers in this genre are already established authors or performers; in their autobiographies they attempt to document their struggles but also to acknowledge the positive forces that enabled them to become recognized writers or artists. This class of autobiographer is concerned with language and tends to be conscious of style and technique. Angelou's forerunners in black literary autobiography include Langston Hughes, *The Big Sea* (1940); W. E. B. Du Bois, *What the Negro Wants* (1944); and James Baldwin, *Notes of a Native Son* (1953).

Although the reader tends to think of Angelou as primarily a singer and entertainer, some of her earliest interests were in language and literature—in the novels of Harlem Renaissance writer Jessie Fauset, in the poetry of Edgar Allan Poe. Her passion for poetry, art, and dance follows her through her autobiographies. It is not until the fourth volume,

though, that Angelou starts to describe herself as a writer and that she
begins to write performable theatrical pieces.

TRAVEL NARRATIVES: DREAMING OF AFRICA

Like other autobiographical works, Angelou's autobiographies are a
mixture of several genres. In her case, autobiography is interlaced, especially in the fourth and fifth volumes, with travel narrative, a classification that is popular among black writers, many of whom went to
Africa and recorded their quest for identity or their achievement of self-
enlightenment. Of the twentieth-century black writers who recorded
their travels in Africa, Langston Hughes provides the prototype in *The
Big Sea* (1940). Hughes, who grew up in Kansas, longed for the faraway
place of Africa. He traveled to the land of his desires in 1923, sailing
there as a merchant seaman. Seeing Africa, Hughes salutes her as the
"Motherland of the Negro Peoples" and "the great Africa of my
Dreams!" terms similar to some of Angelou's praises of Ghana in *All
God's Children Need Traveling Shoes*.

In a comprehensive essay on travel narrative, Mary G. Mason docu-
ments the journeys of Nancy Prince, Ida B. Wells, Eslanda Goode Robeson, Gwendolyn Brooks, Maya Angelou, and other black women writers
who took the long African journey or the shorter one in the Caribbean.
Mason contends that the historic journey taken by previous black women
has become, for modern writers like Angelou, a pilgrimage that reveals
their African heritage. Angelou's 1986 travel narrative, *All God's Children
Need Traveling Shoes*, is part of a genre that "adds a unique theme to
women's autobiographical traditions" (1990, 355).

John C. Gruesser, in his 1990 study of travel narrative, provides a
negative overview of how certain African American writers have dis-
paraged the image of Africa, showing the continent as blank, empty, and
formless, as "a swamp, a question mark" (7). Gruesser discusses the
image of Africa in Richard Wright's *Black Power* (1954), Gwendolyn
Brooks's *Report from Part One* (1972), and Maya Angelou's *All God's Children Need Traveling Shoes* (1986), claiming that each of these African
American writers portrays Africa "either as a dream or a nightmare" (9).
They are disappointed when the Africa of their travels fails to equal the
Africa of their imaginations. Gruesser argues that Angelou, although she
searches for an African connection in Ghana, fails to achieve the goal.
Instead, she forms her primary relationships among African American

expatriates who share romanticized views of Africa as mother. Like many Americans in Africa, they base their experience on distorted images rather than reality.

Using the narrative structure of the black American who goes to Africa, Angelou and other writers reverse the order of history. Where black Africans were once brought in bondage to America, so black Americans retrace the journey back to Africa, their travel books become reflections of the impact that African captivity and African nationhood have had on their own lives.

One final narrative that needs to be mentioned in this context is Marita Golden's *Migrations of the Heart* (1983), a love story written in the first person. Golden's title, with its telltale heart, is enough to prove Gruesser's point that black American women who first encounter Africa are living out fantasies, based on romantic images. A New Yorker, Golden migrates to Africa to be with Femi, the Nigerian lover she met in Manhattan at a social event. Like Angelou's initial relationship with Vusumzi Make, Golden's romance with Femi, the handsome Nigerian, is based primarily on being fulfilled by a man. After one miscarriage, Marita gives birth to Tunde, the valued firstborn son. But she is unhappy, especially when Femi starts to beat her. Unable to adapt to Nigerian life, especially to the bonding among brothers and to the economic obligations demanded from the extended family, Golden returns to America, taking her son with her.

Golden's *Migrations of the Heart*, was published in 1983, three years before the publication of Angelou's fifth volume, *All God's Children Need Traveling Shoes*. Although there are some similarities, such as the loss of community that pervades both narratives, Golden's Nigeria is presented from a woman's perspective, with the emphasis on miscarriage, childbirth, and marriage. These autobiographical themes, while focusing on West African society, might have occurred in any urban setting that had inadequate housing and medical care.

SLAVE NARRATIVES

Historical Roots

Autobiographies written before the Civil War have taken numerous forms, among them traveler's narratives, diaries, success stories, Indian narratives, and religious confessions (Sayre 1980, 146–47). African American autobiography has its historical roots in still another genre, the slave narrative. Through this method of speaking and writing, slaves recalled the harrowing journey from Africa to America and the atrocities of plantation life. It is a genre that Stephen Butterfield (1974) and many other critics believe to be the foundation of African American autobiographical tradition and a genre that many contemporary writers, Angelou among them, have incorporated into their fiction, their autobiographies, their drama, their poetry.

The slave narrative is structured in the form of a journey, from Africa to America or to some other unchosen location in the African diaspora— a term used to describe the scattering of black people during the slave trade. The concept of the journey is as old as song, as old as literature. Homer used the journey of the Greek hero, Odysseus, to establish a sequence of events in his classical epic *The Odyssey*, recorded around 850 B.C. The journey is an integral structure in the West African epic *Son-Jara* (ca. 1300) and in various Indian epics such as the *Ramayana* (ca. 550 B.C.) and the *Mahabharata* (ca. 400 B.C.).

In its earliest expression, the slave narrative was the recollection by a former slave of his/her struggle in crossing the Atlantic from Africa to America. Some critics claim the first printed narrative was Briton Hammon's account of his suffering and deliverance, published in Boston in 1760; others give credit to James Albert Ukawsaw Gronniosaw for writing the first slave narrative, *An African Prince*, in 1770 (Preface *Norton Anthology of African American Literature* 1997). Traditionally, the slave narrative traced the journey of a slave or former slave of African descent in his/her quest for freedom. Freedom for many narrators meant more than release from the imprisoning system of slavery; it also meant the opportunity to write or print their stories and at the same time denounce the institution that had bound them.

Of the written narratives, many celebrated the achievement of literacy—of being able to read and write—as a major theme. Literacy was equated in the slave's mind with liberation, whereas illiteracy, was a form of bondage enforced by slave owners and overseers. William L. Andrews stresses the connection between freedom and literacy: "In the slave narrative the quest is toward freedom from physical bondage and the enlightenment that literacy can offer to the restricted self- and social consciousness of the slave" (1986, 7).

The themes of reading, writing, and freedom are prominent in what many critics consider the classic of the slave narrative, *Narrative of the Life of Frederick Douglass* (1845). Like so many others, Frederick Douglass was writing for a literate white audience, as a man who would be free. He uses the "power of language and persuasion to tell his own story and use it in the liberation of other men and women" (Sayre 1980, 116). In his narrative, Douglas describes being separated from his mother and being constantly mistreated by a host of masters and their hirelings. Frequently, Douglass associates the inhuman conditions of plantation life with his thwarted desire to write: "My feet had been so cracked by the frost, that the pen with which I am writing might be laid in the gashes" (1845, 271). In presenting this harsh example of life under slavery, Douglass is using his pen for the liberation of others.

Selwyn R. Cudjoe (1984) has observed that Angelou, who was consciously writing within an African American autobiographical tradition, often uses the "we" instead of the "I" point of view, moving from the perspective of the single person to that of the group. He contends that, like the slave narrative, her books are more public than private, more concerned with collective experience than with subjective concerns. Angelou, who is aware of her collective point of view, told one interviewer that she is always trying to convert the first-person singular into the first-person plural (Plimpton 1994, 77).

The emphasis on collectivity is especially relevant to *I Know Why the Caged Bird Sings*, with its church gatherings and its communal bonding. This form of identification within the group is a major aspect of black survival. Angelou has frequently admitted Frederick Douglass's influence on her writings, most significantly in her essay "Mother and Freedom," which alludes to Douglass's mother "enslaved on the plantation eleven miles from her infant son." She would walk to him over this vast distance and then return to her own quarters, trying to convey her love (*Stars* 47–49).

Editor Henry Louis Gates Jr. (1987) is convinced that Douglass's great narrative of 1845 was influenced by an earlier text, *The Interesting Narrative of the Life of Olaudah Equiano* (1789), the story of an African also known as Gustavas Vassa whose enslaved condition began in Guinea, the country of his birth. The strong style and vivid verbal patterns make Equiano's account similar both to the Douglass narrative and to the Angelou series. Frederick Douglass's more limited journey begins in Maryland and ends in New Bedford, Massachusetts, a seaport on the same Atlantic Ocean but several hundred miles farther north. Douglass notes that there are no signs of slavery and that the workers of New Bedford have not been beaten. Here he is able to enjoy the great pleasures of freedom and employment. When he has enough money he subscribes to the abolitionist newspaper, the *Liberator*. Thus, a slave narrative begun in bondage ends in the double reward of freedom and literacy. It is reading that takes him to the meeting halls and eventually to a publisher to recount his story about being a slave.

Whereas Douglass's adventures are geographically restricted, Angelou's adventures occupy an enlarged, almost boundless space. Her tale begins in Stamps, Arkansas, but extends from St. Louis to California, from Africa to Europe, from Cairo to Berlin. In a sense, Angelou's voyage reiterates the enormous sweep of Equiano's voyage, which begins where Angelou's ends, in West Africa. At the beginning of the narrative Equiano is captured while playing with his beloved sister. Their only consolation was in "being in one another's arms all that night, and bathing each other with tears" (1789, 26). The children are temporarily confined in Africa. But when the slave boats arrive, Equiano and his sister are forever separated. The intensity of their friendship is not unlike the relationship between Maya and her brother Bailey. Abandoned by their parents, Maya and Bailey gathered strength from each other during their childhood in Stamps.

Equiano describes the horror and stench of the ship, the "loathsome smells" from sickness and filth. Because of his youth and agility, he is spared the lower deck, where slaves are chained together and die together. Equiano's captivity carries him from Guinea, to Canada, to the Mediterranean, the Arctic, Central America, the West Indies, the East Coast of America, and numerous other locations. The voyage culminates in London with his conversion to Christianity, much as Angelou's concludes in West Africa with her acceptance of a dual heritage and Douglass's ends with his commitment to the liberation of his people.

In an emotional sense, though, Angelou's narrative is more restricted than either Douglass's or Equiano's, more maternal and more internalized. In its female preoccupations it has much in common with the slave narrative known as *Incidents in the Life of a Slave Girl* (1861), written by Harriet Jacobs under the pseudonym Linda Brent. Brent's very title and authorship indicate the absence of name, the absence of a serious narrative; her title does not introduce the adventures of specific men—Frederick Douglass or Briton Hammon or Olaudah Equiano—but of "a Slave Girl." Her story does not tell "the life of" or "the interesting narrative of" but only "incidents in." This nonetheless powerful narrative is discussed in Chapter 7 as the paramount example of how the African American slave narrative relates to Angelou's autobiographical series.

Contemporary Applications

Angelou's narrative combines two distinct characteristics of the slave narrative: It demonstrates both the narrative of movement, as represented by Olaudah Equiano, and also the narrative of confinement, a theme common to all imprisoned slave narrators, but having a special significance for women, who were more concerned with the problems of sexual exploitation, rape, loss of dignity, and forsaken children than were male slaves because under the slave system the nuclear family structure was discouraged or forbidden or disrupted when a slave was sold. Deborah E. McDowell (1993) argues that among male slave narrators like Frederick Douglass there is a flagrant disregard for women's issues such as rape, child care, and the stability of the family.

Like the nineteenth-century female slave narrator, Maya Angelou charts her journey toward autonomy. Abandoned by her parents, raped by her mother's boyfriend, separated from her grandmother, the young Maya is imprisoned and unable to claim her own identity. Her journey toward self-discovery takes her from ignorance to knowledge, from silence to speech, from racial oppression to a liberated life, as she travels from Stamps, Arkansas, to Accra, Ghana, and back to America. Her story thus echoes the course of the slave narrative, with its movement from Africa to America, its account of the cruelties of slavery, and its ultimate hope for emancipation.

For Angelou, who writes a personal version of the Emancipation Proclamation, her demoralizing childhood experiences with racial bigotry and sexual assault are largely overcome as she continues her efforts to be somebody—a writer, a dancer, a nonslave. In all her autobiographies, but especially in *The Heart of a Woman* and *All God's Children Need Traveling Shoes*, the format of the slave narrative is enhanced through the African settings and the expanse of her journeys. Angelou connects herself to the slave narrative by consciously linking herself to an African-centered tradition. Her triumph owes much to her rediscovery of her African heritage and her ability to redefine herself as mother and woman.

Other black women writers have considered the slave narrative from a contemporary perspective. Critic Hazel V. Carby claims that women's slave narratives "haunt the texts" of contemporary African American women writers (1987, 61), reiterating the themes of humiliation, hunger, and physical abuse. In *Praisesong for the Widow* (1984), Paule Marshall reinvents the story of legendary West African slaves who crossed the Atlantic Ocean to the banks of South Carolina, while in *Beloved* (1987), Toni Morrison reconstructs the narrative of an historic woman slave who murdered her baby girl to save her from slavery. In her 1989 novel, *The Temple of My Familiar*, Alice Walker's heroine fantasizes the ordeals of the horrendous journey in slave ships, where nursing mothers shared their milk with children who were starving. Marshall, Walker, and Morrison, like other black women writers of the twentieth century, offer parallels between their stories and the slave narratives. Like them, Angelou recognizes in her own life story elements inherent in the genre, such as isolation, abuse, and the absence of home and community.

THE SPIRITUAL

Another prominent influence on Angelou's work is the Negro spiritual, a musical form that originated during the "Great Revival" meetings of the early nineteenth century. This music grew from Protestant camp meetings that were attended by both whites and blacks. During the 1920s and 1930s people like art historian Alain Locke, singer Paul Robeson, and anthropologist Zora Neale Hurston were dedicated to promoting the Negro spiritual as a pure, artistic form. It was Hurston's position that a spiritual could not be performed by a college choir: "The real Negro singer cares nothing about pitch" or other technical matters, Hurston argued. In the genuine spiritual, every singer is "fired by the same inner urge" (qtd. in Hemenway 1977, 56).

In an interview Angelou responded to a question about the title of *Traveling Shoes* by singing several lines from a Negro spiritual: "I've got shoes, you got shoes / All of God's children got shoes" ("Icon" 1997). Angelou utilizes the spiritual for its thematic and symbolic connotations in presenting one of her major themes, her transformational journey to Africa and back.

The Negro spiritual frequently contains the dual motifs of travel and race—of traveling to freedom and escaping the racial bondage of slavery. Angelou, who was moved by an "inner urge," sang parts of three different spirituals during the "Icon" interview. Her attitude toward the genre is delightfully unacademic: "If they are songs about the spirit, then they are gospel songs. Some they call gospel and some spirituals. But those are just titles which help people to codify for the Dewey Decimal System or something. The people who wrote them and sang them, they thought they were all spirituals."

Perhaps the best illustration of her use of the spiritual occurs in *Traveling Shoes*, during her meeting in Cairo with William V. S. Tubman, who was the president of Liberia from 1943 to 1971 (Liberia was founded in the early 19th century by a society wanting to provide homes for slaves who returned to the African continent after achieving their emancipation). Tubman, recalling and naming his American African heritage, requests that she sing a Negro spiritual, "Swing Low, Sweet Chariot." The chariot to the promised land is a symbol that reinforces the travel motif and places Angelou's text within the African American oral tradition. She employs the genre to foreshadow her cultural return from an African identity to an African American one, and to signify her connection with her Southern heritage.

Like the slave narrative, but on a lesser scale, the Negro spiritual also traces the journey from slavery to freedom. In the slave narrative, freedom is achieved within the boundaries of an autobiographical text, whereas in the spiritual, freedom is postponed until arriving in the heavenly kingdom of the New Jerusalem. The spiritual is a collective outcry in a form repeated over and over, whereas autobiography is an individual recollection, often with the collective or "we" point of view. Other examples of the Negro spiritual include the slaves' journey to the Biblical river in "Roll, Jordan, Roll" or to the restored kingdom of Zion in "Sabbath Has No End" (Southern 1971, 201–2). Ironically, a number of religious travel songs had a practical value, since many were encoded with directions for escape.

POETRY

Maya Angelou: A Critical Companion is a study of Angelou's autobiographies. Her sizable body of poetry, while not under specific examination in this work, is relevant to her autobiographical themes and has greatly contributed to her popularity as a contemporary writer. While James Weldon Johnson and Frederick Douglass may have shaped her views about black narrative structures, it should also be emphasized that many of her literary heroes were poets, white and black, male and female. They influenced the way she wrote, thought, and imagined.

As a child, Angelou was affected by the ideas and rhythms of lyric poetry. In *Caged Bird* she is quite specific in acknowledging her debt to William Shakespeare, Edgar Allan Poe, and James Weldon Johnson. In the "Icon" interview of June 16, 1997, Angelou insisted that black women poets also affected her, although she does not acknowledge their influence in *Caged Bird*. She mentioned Georgia Douglas Johnson, a poet who wrote with emotion about gender and from whom she took the title of her fourth autobiography, *The Heart of a Woman*. Other black women poets Angelou admired when she was young were Frances Harper and Anne Spencer: "Frances Harper meant a lot to me. Georgia Douglas Johnson. Anne Spencer. And Jessie Fauset" ("Icon"). Of these women writers, three were known as poets although Harper (1825–1911), is also remembered for her novels, especially for *Iola Leroy* (1895), the story of a woman of mixed race. Angelou quotes from Frances Harper's poem, "The Slave Auction," in one of the reflections that appears in *Even the Stars Look Lonesome* (42). Georgia Douglas Johnson wrote "The Heart of a Woman," the 1918 lyric that became the title of Angelou's fourth autobiography. Anne Spencer (1882–1975) appealed to Angelou for her poignant ballad, "Lady, Lady" (1925), about a servant whose hands had been bleached white from detergent, and for other ballads illustrating the oppression of black women. Finally, novelist Jessie Fauset (1884–1961) was literary editor of *The Crisis*, founded by W.E.B. Du Bois, a renowned black intellectual. Fauset was the most prolific novelist of the Harlem Renaissance (1919–1929), and one of its most educated spokespersons. It is possible that from Fauset Angelou obtained models for plot construction and character development, especially Fauset's reliance on the mother/child motif.

When she was young, Angelou was intrigued by several white women poets. She appreciated the romantic and lyrical qualities of Emily Dickinson (1830–1886), and echoes of Dickinson's familiar ballad form can be heard in some of Angelou's poems. She also enjoyed the passion of Edna St. Vincent Millay (1892–1950) and the caustic humor of Dorothy Parker (1893–1967): "They are funny and wry," she remarked in appreciation of Millay and Parker. "I'm rarely wry. I think I'm funny. I love to be funny" ("Icon" 1997).

When asked about the influence of African and Asian poets on her work she clearly acknowledged Kwesi Brew, the Ghanaian poet who appears in *All God's Children Need Traveling Shoes*: "Oh yes," she said, "Kwesi influenced me and still does. But the early influences, I had no idea African poets even existed early on." She explained that African poets were not published in the United States while she was growing up. One of the first African poets who came to her attention was Sene-galese statesman Leopold Senghor, and that was not until she was an adult ("Icon" 1997). She was more familiar with Chinese and Japanese poets than with African poets because they were available. Some of her poetry has been influenced by the Japanese haiku, a poetic description written in three lines totalling seventeen syllables (Harmon and Holman 1996, 241).

Angelou's autobiographies are informed not only by her experiments in poetic form but also by her journey into Asian, African, and African American literature. In her view, anyone who emerges from the journey of life is an autobiographer. She thus draws all of God's children into her encompassing definition of what makes an autobiographer: "Each one is an autobiographer. . . . So I think we're all on journeys, according to how we're able to travel, overcome, undercome, and share what we have learned" ("Icon" 1997).

3

I Know Why the Caged Bird Sings
(1970)

In 1970 a child with skinny legs and muddy skin was introduced into African American autobiography. Born Marguerite Johnson, she became known as Maya Angelou, an actress and dancer who performed in George Gershwin's musical, *Porgy and Bess*, and in Jean Genet's satirical French play, *The Blacks*; who, two years before, in 1968, wrote a series on African heritage for educational television. Angelou, well known as an entertainer, was urged by James Baldwin and by the cartoonist Jules Feiffer and his wife Judy to try her hand at writing an autobiography. After several refusals she agreed; the result was a unique series of autobiographical narratives.

I Know Why the Caged Bird Sings is the first of Maya Angelou's five autobiographies. It covers her life from the age of three, when her parents send her and her brother Bailey to live with their paternal grandmother, Annie Henderson, in Stamps, Arkansas, until the age of sixteen, when she becomes a mother. Annie Henderson is the main influence on her childhood.

When Maya and Bailey are eight and nine, respectively, they travel to St. Louis, where their mother, Vivian Baxter, and their maternal grandmother are leading a far more sophisticated life than anything Maya had known in Arkansas. There are more parties and fewer church gatherings. In the loose atmosphere of St. Louis, Maya is raped by her mother's boyfriend, Mr. Freeman, who warns her to be silent (mute) or he will kill her brother Bailey. After the trial Freeman dies after being violently beaten, presumably by Maya's uncles. Maya is indeed silent, mute. She cannot/will not speak. The silent Maya is returned to Momma Henderson, remaining speechless for five years until she recovers her voice through the patient help of her grandmother's friend, Mrs. Bertha Flowers.

As Maya emerges from the traumas of childhood, she gains strength from reading literature, and graduates with honors from the eighth grade. Soon after graduation, she and Bailey move to San Francisco, where their mother, Vivian, was living with her new husband, Daddy Clidell. There, Maya simultaneously attends George Washington High School and on a part-time basis, a Marxist labor school. At the latter she takes courses in dance and theater that will prove invaluable in her career.

Worried that she might be a lesbian, she engages in sex with a young man from the neighborhood to disprove her fears. The sixteen-year-old girl, supported financially and emotionally by her parents, gives birth to a son, who becomes the focus of the remaining four autobiographies.

NARRATIVE POINT OF VIEW

Autobiography is generally written from the first-person point of view, the "I," but while the norm, it has occasionally been modified. For example, both Jamaica Kincaid, in *An Autobiography of My Mother* (1996), and Maxine Hong Kingston, in *The Woman Warrior* (1976), recount their lives from the viewpoint of their mothers. James McBride, in *The Color of Water* (1996), uses a double first-person point of view: his own autobiographical account is printed in Roman type and his mother's, also first person, is printed in italics. Through this technique, McBride is able to represent the connections and antagonisms between African American son and Jewish mother.

I Know Why the Caged Bird Sings and the four succeeding volumes use the first-person narrative voice, even though there are many moments that sound more like fiction than autobiography. *Caged Bird* is told by a child who is artfully recreated by the adult narrator. From a child's perspective, Maya records her separation from her mother and father, and her strong religious and communal connections, shared with her paternal grandmother. Revealing her life story through a narrator who is a Southern black female who is at times a child, at times a mother, Maya Angelou introduces a unique point of view to American autobiography.

In classic American autobiographies—those written, for example, by the inventor/statesman Benjamin Franklin (1708–1790), or by Harvard professor Henry Adams (1838–1918)—the narrative is relayed by white men with sound family backgrounds and unlimited educational opportunities. The narrator's purpose in writing his story is to impart a model for living. The memoirs of statesmen such as Winston Churchill (1874–1965), prime minister of England during the Second World War, would also fit this category.

In Angelou's case, the story is told from the unlikely perspective of a black Southern female whose chances to be someone were dreadfully limited, due to the constraints placed on the lives of African American people. And yet she is articulate, sarcastic, upsetting—not at all the kind of narrator that a frequent reader of autobiography expects. From the first moment, she records being underprivileged, an undesirable outsider. According to Sidonie Ann Smith, any black autobiographer will reveal his or her oppression in those earliest moments: "In Black American autobiography the opening almost invariably recreates the environment of enslavement from which the black self seeks escape" (1973, 367). Maya feels ugly, awkward, and is poorly dressed throughout the entire first volume, although she does have flashes of self-pride, for example when she believes that Momma Henderson is rewarding good behavior by putting her and Bailey in the front pew of the Christian Methodist Episcopal Church. Generally, though, she considers her "black self" to be the cage that entraps her.

Similar negative self-perceptions are frequent in black female autobiography, for example in the raw first line of Zora Neale Hurston's *Dust Tracks on a Road* (1942): "Like the dead-seeming, cold rocks, I have memories within that came out of the material that went to make me" (3). For Angelou, the negative sense of self continues into the fourth volume, *The Heart of a Woman*, where she learns to appreciate more fully her changing character.

As the first-person narrator, Angelou is able to tell her unique story while at the same time sharing the contributions of black writers who came before her. From the first moments of *Caged Bird*, she establishes communication with earlier African American art forms: with the poetry of James Weldon Johnson; with the Negro spiritual; with the slave narratives of Frederick Douglass and Harriet Jacobs (Linda Brent). In that sense, the point of view becomes a collective one, the voice not only of the single autobiographer but also of the African American literary community. Dolly A. McPherson (1990), views the collective ties with the black community as a central theme in Angelou's autobiographies, while Elizabeth Fox-Genovese writes of the "collective identity of African American women" within the Southern landscape and in the works of Zora Neale Hurston and Maya Angelou (1990, 222).

STRUCTURE

Structure relates to the shape of a narrative, to its overall design or patterns. C. Hugh Holman and William Harmon define structure as "the planned framework of a piece of literature," determined by features like language, formal divisions, and organization (459). The "planned framework" in Angelou's autobiographies is the concept of a journey or journeys—from south to north; from west to east to west; from place to place in the United States or across the Atlantic Ocean. In *Caged Bird*, the journey is a triangular one, almost like having a set of three thumbtacks—a map of the United States to represent California and Arkansas and Missouri. If the tacks are moved as the character Maya moves in the book, a reader can get a solid sense of how structure operates within an autobiographical text.

Each of Angelou's autobiographies relies on movement as equivalent to travel; the movement from journey to journey establishes the narrative line. In recording her momentous journey Angelou, without being directly repetitive, constantly recreates and rewinds the structure, replaying it at different speeds and at different volumes. The idea of movement is extensive in the autobiographies, beginning with the denial of movement on the first page of *Caged Bird*—"I didn't come to stay"—to the word "traveling," which dominates the title of the fifth volume, *All God's Children Need Traveling Shoes*.

In writing *I Know Why the Caged Bird Sings*, Angelou chooses the train ride from California to Arkansas to represent the beginning of her autobiographical journey. Eugenia Collier notes that Angelou's use of the journey is on one level an escape from an impossible circumstance, while "on another level, each is a further step in Maya's journey toward awareness" (1986, 22). Of other journeys within the triad, the trip to St. Louis in her father's car is the most terrible for in St. Louis she is raped by her mother's boyfriend. Years later, in a journey to Mexico, this same father is present as the travel patterns again assume a sinister tone. Maya, who has never been behind the wheel of a car, maneuvers her father's car fifty miles down the mountainside because he is too drunk to drive. After she is stabbed by her father's girlfriend, she moves to a vacant lot and stays with a number of multiethnic teenagers who are also running away from unacceptable living situations. In that particular section of the book, the sense of movement—driving, stabbing, running, running away, bumping, yelling—becomes overwhelming.

Following this jolting series of events, Maya returns to Vivian and, in a desperate plan to prove she is a woman, becomes pregnant by a neighborhood boy. On the day she graduates from the summer school of Mission High School, still living in San Francisco with Vivian Baxter and Daddy Clidell, Maya leaves a note on their bed informing them that she is pregnant. After her mother and step-father assuage Maya's fears, the mother-to-be slows down. In the quiet conclusion of *Caged Bird*, Maya lies in bed with her baby, her mother present, in a tableau of stillness that suggests the Nativity scene. Angelou conveys the sacredness of motherhood here and in an earlier comment that she had had an "immaculate pregnancy" (245), preparing the stage for the blessed journey into motherhood that will be the underlying theme for the next four volumes.

PLOT DEVELOPMENT

A successful plot is a whole; it contains a beginning, a middle, and an end, each connected to the other. In autobiography, plot is far less necessary, since it is concerned with the concept of the self rather than with the actions the self performs. In autobiography it becomes difficult to draw the line between character (the one who acts) and plot (the action of the story). The two elements tend to fuse together, with plot becoming dependent on the feelings and mannerisms of the narrator.

Yet as many critics have maintained, the plot of an autobiography must, like the plot of a novel, have a beginning, a middle, and an end. For the novel, the ending can be contrived or implausible, wild or fanciful, since the novel is not guided by the dictates of rationality.

For autobiography to be of value, the ending must be consistent with the beginning and the middle. In other words, the ending must occur within the predictable limits of what the author has already revealed to the reader. Angelou ends *Caged Bird* with the altogether believable scene of Maya, her own mother at her side, lying in bed with her baby, afraid that if she falls asleep she will roll over on her infant. No fireworks, but a lot of feeling. Few readers realized, when they read this touching last scene in 1970, that the sleeping baby represented not only the end of *Caged Bird* but the beginning of Angelou's serial autobiography. The question of how an autobiography ends is examined in each of the subsequent chapters of this work.

The plot of *Caged Bird* begins when Maya and her brother Bailey arrive in Stamps, Arkansas, to live with their paternal grandmother and her crippled son, Willie. It covers thirteen years of chronological time, from Maya's third to sixteenth year. Of the various incidents in the plot that have a negative effect on Maya, two of them are extremely disruptive: being raped on a visit to St. Louis at the age of eight, and becoming pregnant as a result of trying to prove to herself that she is not a lesbian.

Angelou's recounting of the rape and its aftermath is brilliantly done. One might contrast Maya's rape to John Grisham's depiction of child molestation and rape in *A Time to Kill* (1992). Grisham's fictional account, though, for all its graphic detail, is told from the perspective of a white male lawyer and not, as in *Caged Bird*, from the personal experience of a black female child. Grisham the novelist is removed from the event, while Angelou the autobiographer is painfully present.

The rape scene, so powerful in its physical and emotional impact, contains narrative elements that are magnified to the extent that the reader might think of the rape as the essence of plot. Maya's stained panties, Mr. Freeman's "cold face and empty eyes" (67), Maya's outburst in court—each of these details is loaded with action. Ironically, for Maya, the rape is the ultimate learning experience. Through her pain she becomes aware of being a small girl in a world controlled by men. The violation to her undeveloped body and the guilt she feels when her uncles evidently kick Mr. Freeman to death create a negative chain of events followed by five years of silence as Maya refuses to speak. She is finally restored to language by her close relationship with Mrs. Bertha Flowers, a learned friend of her grandmother's, who liberates Maya from her wordless cavern.

The second major event in the plot is Maya's decision to test her femininity by having sex, an action that results in pregnancy. For many young women, a teenage pregnancy might end in trauma, abortion, or parental rejection. For Maya, the pregnancy ends in her mother's acceptance and the birth of her son. Sidonie Ann Smith connects the ending and the birth to Maya's affirmation of self: "With the birth of her child

Maya is herself born into a mature engagement with the forces of life" (1973, 374).

It is this engagement, this birth, that generates character development and theme in the remaining four volumes. Depending on where Maya goes, theme and character build upon the oppositions within the mother/son relationship. No other serial autobiography places the theme of mother and child within the eye of the conflict, making it of supreme importance to the narrative(s).

CHARACTER DEVELOPMENT

Angelou's autobiographies tend to derive their form through the interaction of characters rather than through the development of a dramatic line of action. When Maya and Bailey arrive in Stamps, hungry, alone, and unprotected, their characters lack all substance. They are as empty as the name tags they wear to assert their identities.

In her evolution from child to woman, Maya fills readers' imaginations as have very few similar characters in American autobiography. Alfred Kazin (1964) argues that recreating those early years offers the autobiographer the greatest incentive. Childhood, he contends, is the perfect perspective for revealing the self, in part because the narrator derives pleasure from transferring the informed thoughts of an adult into the imaginative visions of a child. Although he is not writing about Angelou, Kazin's remarks fit her perfectly.

This section investigates Maya's character as a child and young adult, with attention to how she acts and is acted in three specific areas: in the family, in the black community, and in the white community. Maya's performance in these areas reveals the diversity of her character and gives a sense of the various moods, attitudes, and strategies involved in her survival as a black child in a world manipulated by images of whiteness.

Autobiography is a genre designed to be a revelation of the self, as shaped through personal attachments, often with present or absent family members. In *I Know Why the Caged Bird Sings*, Maya's interaction with her mother, brother, son, and grandmother tends to order and solidify her experiences. Although these are all strong relationships, Maya's ties with her grandmother are probably the most important in forming her character.

Momma Henderson is a church-going, God-fearing woman whose

store is the heart of black socializing in Stamps. She has strict ideas about taking God's name in vain and even stricter ones about relating to white folks. Believing in the safe approach, Momma insists that talking to "white-folks" is taking a chance with "one's life" (39). Despite her many strengths, she is a woman who submits to racist behavior without a struggle, maintaining the submissive manners of the past. Maya is unable to accept her grandmother's position that for Southern blacks to survive in a racist society, they must develop a strategy of obedience. She disagrees with Annie Henderson's passive stance but fears how whites might react to Bailey's having witnessed a black man's death at their hands. Annie, fearing white vengeance, sends the children to the safety of California.

There are a number of episodes in which Maya and Momma Henderson disagree about white folks. The most dramatic involves some rural white girls who stand in front of Mama's store and taunt her, like the witches from Macbeth. One of the "powhitetrash" girls brazenly exposes her private parts in a butt-naked handstand to the God-fearing Momma. Symbolically, the adolescent is displaying her white sexuality before Annie Henderson, store owner, a black woman who is unable to respond except through passively humming a spiritual. In his interpretation of this episode, Stephen Butterfield sees Momma's passivity as a victory in self-control (1974, 211), whereas Dolly A. McPherson reads the confrontation as an example of white girls using their power to "treat a Black woman like another child" (1990, 32). Maya, furious at her grandmother's compliance, wishes that she could blow away the problem with a rifle.

In another racist episode, Momma takes Maya to the town's white dentist, who humiliates his black patients by saying that he'd rather put his "hand in a dog's mouth than in a nigger's" (160). In each instance, it is Annie's passivity that disturbs Maya, who is beginning to articulate her anger about racism. Maya's response is to invent a fantasy in which Momma Henderson holds Dentist Lincoln by the collar and orders him to "leave Stamps by sundown" (161). This stock phrase from a western movie grants Annie the male authority that Maya wants her to have: Annie is the hero, and the dentist is the unforgiven villain. The fantasy, printed in italics, is Maya's way of dealing with the dentist's racist behavior and with her grandmother's inability to question his racism.

It hurts Maya to see her grandmother humiliated by a so-called professional who is unworthy, who even owes her interest payments on a loan. These humiliating situations cause Maya to feel confused toward Momma Henderson, who represents conflicting qualities: She is both strong and weak, courageous and fearful, caring and cold. Angelou exaggerates Annie's power, recalling that Momma Henderson—over six feet tall—was "taller than any woman in my personal world" (38); to Maya her physical strength is unequaled. Mildred A. Hill-Lubin, who argues for the cultural importance of the black grandmother in African and African American communities, selects Annie Henderson as a grandmother who represents physical strength and the "stability and the continuity of the Black family and the community" (1986, 257). Although Momma becomes Maya's source of knowledge, values, and morality, she is still troubled by her grandmother's opinions about language, race, and white writers such as Shakespeare, Maya's "first white love" (11). When they recite poetry for Momma, Maya and Bailey are careful to choose the black poet James Weldon Johnson instead of the dead, white Shakespeare.

Uncle Willie, Annie Henderson's son, has been under her special care since he was a child, crippled at the age of three when a babysitter dropped him. Willie walks with a cane to support his disfigured body. In an early scene, Maya-witnesses Momma burying Uncle Willie in a large bin, under layers of potatoes and onions, to avoid being detected by the Ku Klux Klan. Still, Uncle Willie has an active role in running the store, which is the hub of the black community. He handles the sales on the night of the heavy-weight championship between the famed black boxer, Joe Louis (1914–1981), and a white man. All of black Stamps gather at Annie's store to watch the historic fight. Men and women living under the yoke of racism think that if Louis loses "we were back in slavery and beyond help" (113).

In the film version of *I Know Why the Caged Bird Sings*, directed by Fielder Cook, there is a touching scene between Willie and Maya that occurs after the fight is over. Joe Louis has won and Uncle Willie feels that he has been redeemed, that he, too, is a man who can stand up to whites. Although Uncle Willie's sentiments are, strangely, not conveyed in Angelou's book, they are beautifully presented in the film in dialogue between Maya and her uncle that adds depth to his character.

After Momma Henderson, Maya's brother Bailey is the family member who has the greatest influence on her young life. He is bright, clever, and good-spirited. Maya measures people by her small-framed brother, her hero, her "Kingdom Come" (19). For five years Vivian has ignored Maya and Bailey, at times trying to buy their affection by sending presents. During their estrangement from Vivian Baxter, Maya learns to cope by putting her trust into the strong hands of Annie Henderson and the reliable good feelings of her brother.

One day Bailey Sr. arrives from California to take them on a journey. After the trip has started, he announces that they are going to see their mother. Vivian has left California and is living in St. Louis, Missouri, with the Baxter family, headed by Grandmother Baxter, a neighborhood precinct leader of German/black descent who has connections with the city police. There are three formidable brothers, Tutti, Tom, and Ira. Maya is in awe of her beautiful mother, a woman "too beautiful to have children" (50). She often describes her mother through images of lightness or floating: for instance, she moved "like a pretty kite that floated just above my head" (54).

Six months later, Vivian and the children move into a house with Mr. Freeman, who works in the Southern Pacific Railway yards. The harmony of the newly-formed family is brutally disrupted, though, when Mr. Freeman rapes Maya. After the rape it is Bailey and not Vivian who is able to comfort Maya; he is her voice and spirit during the years of silence that follow their return to Stamps.

In a powerful episode Bailey comes home to Momma Henderson shaken and pale. He saw a dead, bloated black man, covered with a sheet, pulled from the water. A white man ordered Bailey and some colored men to put the corpse into a jail filled with prisoners. Confused and unable to understand why white people could have such hatred of blacks, Bailey gets no answers from his grandmother or his uncle.

Bailey's encounter with the dead man prompts Momma Henderson to send the children to Vivian Baxter, who has since left St. Louis and returned to California. In a poignant image that emphasizes the geographical distance between California and Arkansas and between mother and children, Maya imagines a mother who could never "laugh and eat oranges in the sunshine without her children" (42).

Again on a train, Maya and Bailey return to Vivian Baxter. Maya is thirteen and Bailey a year older. Vivian captivates both children with her worldliness and elation. Not until her early twenties does Maya see herself as having separated herself emotionally from her mother. She told novelist Rosa Guy, "I began to see her as a character I would have read about" (1989, 221).

Maya's father, Bailey Sr., is less prominent than Vivian Baxter in shaping Maya's character. He represents the absent father, the man who is not there for his children, literally and figuratively. This figure is prevalent in American literature, among urban and rural, poor and middle-class, black and white families. Maya sees her father only twice in *I Know Why the Caged Bird Sings*—in his initial appearance when he drives his children to St. Louis, and a second time when Maya visits him for a bizarre summer vacation in southern California. In neither instance is he able to show much affection for his daughter.

In her father's absence, Maya finds substitute father figures, men like Mr. Freeman, who will give her the attention her father cannot, or she makes fun of men so they become undesirable to her. She enjoys joking with Bailey about pompous fatherly types like Reverend Thomas, who visits Annie Henderson to take advantage of her home cooking. Uncle Willie, her father's blood brother, is a substitute father in the strictest sense. At one time, Maya, feeling sorry for her uncle's disability, comments that if he wishes, she would be his make-believe daughter. She admits that Uncle Willie would have been a better father than Bailey Sr. But his speech problems and her insecurity prevent a good relationship from developing between them.

The most apparent father substitute is Mr. Freeman, a man who sits up and waits until Vivian comes home from dealing poker in gambling parlors. When Maya has nightmares, the three of them sleep together. One morning after Vivian gets up, Mr. Freeman touches Maya and pulls her on top of him, his right hand moving rapidly. Maya feels "at home" and imagines that he is her "real father" whom she has finally found (61). While not a member of the family Vivian's live-in boyfriend has a husband's place in Vivian's sex life and a stepfather's role with regard to Vivian's daughter, a trust that he violates in both cases.

When Maya reveals that it was Freeman who raped her, he is put on trial and found guilty. Soon afterwards, Freeman's body is discovered, beaten to death. Maya suspects her uncles. After Maya becomes mute, Vivian is unable to break through her wall of silence. Maya and Bailey are once again returned to Stamps.

The black community of Stamps is an extended family. Through her interaction with the black people of Stamps, Maya develops her character, growing stronger and sharpening her wit by associating with people like Sister Monroe, Reverend Thomas, Mr. McElroy, and Mrs. Flowers. Some of Maya's insights are related to social class. Mr. McElroy is the only black man Maya has ever seen whose trousers match his jackets. She learns that he wears suits, and she claims that suits are good things because when men wear them they look a bit like women, making their appearance less severe. Maya and Bailey admire Mr. McElroy because he doesn't go to church, which makes him "courageous," since he is Annie's neighbor (16).

Almost everyone else in the town is a churchgoer, from Momma Henderson to Deacon Jackson. A great deal of the humor in *Caged Bird* derives from Angelou's caricatures of Southern black folks who've got religion. The funniest episodes involve Sister Monroe, who is not always able to come to the Sunday service. When she does, she shouts as loud as possible to make up for having been absent. One morning when Reverend Taylor is preaching the sermon, Sister Monroe starts yelling "Preach it" so loud the church shakes (33). One deacon hits the preacher, who hits another deacon in a chain reaction while Sister Monroe walks calmly from the altar.

Another figure of ridicule is Reverend Thomas, a repulsive church official who comes to Stamps four times a year; on those occasions he eats "like a hog" at the home of Annie Henderson (27). There are several reasons why Maya and Bailey despise Reverend Thomas: He is obese; he never remembers their names; and worst of all, he eats the very best pieces of chicken at Sunday dinner. He, too, becomes Sister Monroe's victim when one Sunday while he is preaching she hits him so hard on the head with her purse that his teeth fly onto the floor near Maya and Bailey. At this point the children roll on the floor, laughing hysterically until Uncle Willie takes them next door to a church building and gives them "the whipping of our lives" (37).

Of all of the black residents of Stamps, the one person Angelou treats with unqualified respect is Mrs. Bertha Flowers. Maya calls her the "aristocrat of Black Stamps" (77). A self-supporting, independent, graceful woman, Mrs. Flowers gently nurses Maya through her years of silence by reading to her and loaning her books so that Maya's love of literature makes her want to speak it. The critic Mary G. Mason (1990), although she doesn't specify Angelou, has observed a pattern in women's autobiographies in which another woman—a mother, a daughter, a grandmother, a friend—helps the subject identify herself as a writer. This pattern certainly holds true for Mrs. Flowers, whose encouragement is a major factor in Maya's development as reader, autobiographer, and poet.

Through her experiences with the strong women of Stamps, Maya "links herself to the Southern roots and history of her people—to a succession of American Negro female survivors" (Fox-Genovese 1990, 230). Her involvement with the black community in church, at the store, at picnics, empowers Angelou, enabling her to understand the rules for survival in a racist society. Through her growing racial awareness, she is able to articulate her observations of racism, if not aloud then at least in her thoughts. Thus, she can witness the Joe Louis fight and fear that in his possible defeat each blow to Louis's body is like a black man being beaten or a black maid being slapped for being "forgetful" (113). It is many years before Angelou is able to put such thoughts into spoken words to share with white and black audiences.

The episodes concerning the "powhitetrash" girls and Dentist Lincoln provide apt examples of Maya's reaction to the racism coming from the white community. As an historical document, *I Know Why the Caged Bird Sings* captures the vulgarity of white Southern attitudes toward African Americans. Angelou presents this material by recalling racist characters so real that one can feel their presence—Mr. Donleavy, Mrs. Cullinan, and other whites whose bigotry dramatically affects Maya's childhood and leaves such a scar on the mature Maya Angelou that when she finally returns to Stamps in 1982 to film an interview with Bill Moyers, she refuses to cross the bridge into the white part of town. This discussion of Maya's character development follows the example of Stamps in dividing the black and white communities along racial lines to reflect the divisions that were there when Angelou was a child and that presumably still are there.

Of the whites who affect Maya's character, one is Mrs. Viola Cullinan, a woman Maya works for when she is ten. Mrs. Cullinan has a vast array of cups and glasses, including the ones set aside for the servants. The woman treats Maya as though she does not exist, calling her Mary or Margaret instead of her given name, Marguerite. As Maya explains, whites called black people too many other names for centuries for her to tolerate Mrs. Cullinan's abuse. Maya tries to get fired by coming late to work, but to no avail. One day, in a moment of anger, she smashes several pieces of Mrs. Cullinan's prized china. Dolly A. McPherson sees Maya's intentional breaking of Mrs. Cullinan's china as an affirmation of Maya's "individuality and value." The confrontation is necessary if Maya is to save herself from the "dehumanizing atmosphere of her environment" (1990, 45).

Another white whose bigotry affects Maya is Mr. Donleavy, the guest speaker at the eighth-grade graduation at the segregated Lafayette County Training School. Amid all of the pride and loving detail that surround Angelou's exquisite description of graduation day, Mr. Donleavy hangs over the event like a dense white cloud. All his ideas about education are formed along divisions of race and gender. Some first-rate baseball and football players once graduated from Lafayette County Training School, he remarks, never mentioning the black girls. He is pleased that because of his efforts, the white students at Central High School will be getting new microscopes for their laboratories. When Donleavy leaves for a more pressing obligation, having destroyed the educational dreams of the black children, Henry Reed, the valedictorian, turns to the audience and starts singing the Negro national anthem.

Angelou, who wrote the script for the film version of *I Know Why the Caged Bird Sings*, presents the graduation scene quite differently, making Maya more central to the episode and making her more rebellious than she is in the book. Maya, not Henry Reed, delivers the valedictory speech. Instead of reading her prepared remarks, she attacks Donleavy's concepts, saying that black boys don't need to be football players and that black girls don't have to be cooks or housekeepers. The audience is at first shocked, and even more so when Maya, not Henry, begins to sing James Weldon Johnson's inspirational Negro national anthem, which had been banned from public ceremonies in the schools. But they gradually join her until their voices rise in a powerful chorus. As the camera pans the faces of the proud black audience, the film ends. Sadly, Maya's triumphant rebuttal of his sexist and racist beliefs was not the reality at the 1940 graduation of the Lafayette County Training School, which occurred two decades before the civil-rights movement and the reluctant integration of public schools.

There are many other white people in *I Know Why the Caged Bird Sings*, people Maya knows through direct exposure, like Mr. Donleavy, or through a general awareness of their power over her life. Most of the men, like Mrs. Cullinan's husband, remain blurred in her memory, like "all the other white men that I had ever seen and tried not to see" (89).

Once she leaves Stamps for the more liberated atmosphere of San Francisco, Maya discovers a few whites who are kind to her. Miss Kirwin, Maya's civics and current events teacher at the predominantly white George Washington High School, is a "rare educator" (182). Although Maya is one of three black students, Miss Kirwin shows no favoritism. She attaches no difference to the fact that Maya is black. The adult narrator confesses that Miss Kirwin was "the only teacher I remembered" (184)—and perhaps the only white person who had ever befriended her.

SETTING

Setting includes such considerations as racial distribution, climate, work environment, and other associated factors. In Angelou's autobiographical series the variety of settings is remarkable, as she sweeps the reader on a magic carpet that flies from Arkansas to Ghana, with stopping points in a number of European capitals. Setting designates how the characters interact. Her rape, for example, would not likely have occurred in Stamps, Arkansas, with its close-knit community and its rigid moral code.

The first side of the triangular setting in *I Know Why the Caged Bird Sings* begins on a train that takes Maya and Bailey to a small Southern town. The setting then moves to St. Louis and San Francisco. In Stamps, Arkansas, she is engulfed with feelings of rejection and abandonment, countered by her love for Momma Henderson and her love of poetry. In Stamps, Maya is naive and innocent. She has fantasies of power involving her grandmother and herself as they conquer racism.

The second side of the triangle is St. Louis, Missouri, where her mother Vivian is a card dealer and her paternal grandmother is a political power in the community. Maya and Bailey attend a large school where the students are so ignorant that the "country children" from Arkansas are moved up a grade. The extended family lives together until Vivian and Mr. Freeman get a house to share with Maya and Bailey. At this juncture, Maya is left vulnerable to assault.

The triangle is completed in San Francisco, the West Coast city which will be the central geographical focus of Angelou's autobiographies until *The Heart of a Woman*. Her mother's home furnishes the final setting, with three generations—Vivian, Maya, and Guy—united in a harmony that belies the separation and abandonment of Maya's beginnings.

THEMATIC ISSUES

The literary theme depends for its effect on the use of repetition. In Maya Angelou's autobiographical series many different themes appear and reappear. The major themes in *I Know Why the Caged Bird Sings* are motherhood, imprisonment, and rape.

Probably the most consistent thematic issue found in Angelou's autobiographies is motherhood. During much of Maya's childhood her own mother is absent, and her conflicting feelings for Vivian Baxter are transferred to others, especially to Annie Henderson.

Although Maya does not become a mother until the end of the autobiography, for most of the book she is concerned with the parenting qualities of Momma Henderson; her brother Bailey; her father, Bailey Sr.; her mother, Vivian Baxter; and other characters who either nurture her or deny her the mothering she craves: people who help her read; who clothe her; who show her the secrets of urban life. While Maya's primary identification in *Caged Bird* is that of a daughter or granddaughter, these roles become secondary at the end of the book, when she becomes a black mother.

The theme of motherhood is one of the central ideas in contemporary literature by black women: There is the mother who murders her infant in Toni Morrison's *Beloved* or the mother who strives for decent housing in Lorraine Hansberry's *A Raisin in the Sun* (1959). According to Daryl C. Dance, the black mother is "a figure of courage, strength, and endurance," a "Madonna" who has brought her race out of bondage and given them life (1979, 131). Mary Burgher writes that black women autobiographers have redeemed black motherhood from the myths of breeder and matriarch—always having babies, always being domineering—by revealing themselves as women who are both mothers and visionaries. Angelou and other autobiographers are "consistently expanding motherhood into a creative and personally fulfilling role" (1979, 115).

A second major theme in *I Know Why the Caged Bird Sings* is imprisonment. Maya constantly feels caged, unable to get away from the homemade dresses she must wear to church, unable to escape the reality of her blackness. She is imprisoned by her job for Mrs. Cullinan and by her limited opportunities in a segregated school system. There are several painful scenes where she and Bailey, trapped in the church service, are conquered by hysterical laughter. At times Maya urinates at her pew as if in defiance of the restrictions imposed on her young body. She is trapped, too, by the bigotry of Stamps, whose town fathers demand that she and all African Americans live in only one section of town and attend only those schools in their part town. Imprisoned inside her body, Maya believes that a "cruel fairy stepmother" has wickedly transformed her from a blonde child to a dark one.

The theme of imprisonment is expressed in the title *I Know Why the Caged Bird Sings*, which Angelou takes from Paul Lawrence Dunbar's 1896 poem, "Sympathy," a poem about a caged bird who beats his wings against the bars. Elizabeth Fox-Genovese writes eloquently about Angelou's image of the cage: "Unbreakable bars closed black communities in upon themselves, denying both the communities and the individuals who composed them access to the surrounding white world. . . . The cages constrained but did not stifle them" (1990, 221–22). The caged bird, a symbol for the chained slave, frequently reappears in Angelou's writings, especially in *The Heart of a Woman*.

Most critics who write about the title tend to underplay the verb *sings*, the last word and the one that creates an upward mood. But *sings* suggests the survival of African Americans through the spiritual, a form examined in Chapter 2. As it is the nature of the caged bird to sing for its supper, so it is said to be the black person's nature to make music while in bondage—to lift every voice and sing; to sing in praise of the Lord. In Dunbar's poem, for instance, the bruised bird sings a prayer to God that he might be released.

Although Angelou develops the singing aspects of *I Know Why the Caged Bird Sings* in her second and third volumes, she only hints at the possibilities of joyful song in the first book. For like a songless bird, Maya gives up all singing, all sound, during the five years that follow her rape. For five years she is mute, locked in a speechless body, as she has willed it. She is liberated from her caged silence only after Mrs. Flowers helps her release her voice. Listening to Mrs. Flowers read aloud, Maya describes the woman's voice as *singing*: "Her voice slid in and curved down through and over the words. She was nearly singing" (84).

A cage, as Georgia Douglas Johnson warns us, restrains not only the black body but also the female black body; a black woman is doubly threatened because of her race and her gender. The third theme, rape, is a concept so forceful that it overwhelms the autobiography, even though it is presented fairly briefly in the text. The theme involves Maya's two sexual experiences with Mr. Freeman. Both scenes are couched in metaphors, allowing her to describe her pain without having to directly speak/write about what she feels. Unable to comprehend the reality of her situation, she invents comparisons that sound like dirty jokes because they really are dirty jokes, played by a frustrated father substitute on an innocent girl.

Maya compares his "thing" to a "brown ear of corn" (61). It feels pulpy like the "inside of a freshly killed chicken" (61). In both instances she compares what she is unsure of, the penis, to objects familiar to her rural upbringing—to corn and to chicken—as if trying to make the strangeness go away and the experience along with it.

The most famous example of this kind of comparison is the camel/needle metaphor. Angelou writes: "The act of rape on an eight-year-old body is a matter of the needle giving because the camel can't" (65). Mary Vermillion (1992), in her reading of the metaphor, associates the passage with the Biblical parable that it is easier for a camel to go through the eye of a needle than for a rich man to enter the kingdom of Heaven. Angelou's "needle" is also a metaphor for how rape must feel to a vulnerable child. If Maya's vagina (her body) is like a needle's eye and Mr.

Freeman's penis is like a camel, then there is a repulsive physical implication behind the metaphor. Angelou has found the appropriate image
to convey the horror of a child's flesh being ripped by an enlarged,
thrusting penis. The child (needle) gives because the rapist (camel) cannot.

LITERARY STYLE

The narrative style in *Caged Bird* is rich, humorous, intense, engaging.
Sometimes Angelou's language is frightening, as in the camel metaphor,
or vicious, as in the white dentist's remark that he'd "rather stick my
hand in a dog's mouth than in a nigger's" (160). Angelou's use of the
tabooed and inhuman word "nigger" is meant to emphasize the clash
between the dentist's presumed profession as healer and the low-level
nature of his language and philosophy.

Another feature of her style, evident in the same dentist's statement
about the dog's mouth, is the use of sharp and direct dialogue to convey
the distinctive language of a character. Dialogue, is a stylistic feature
throughout Angelou's entire autobiographical series. It seems most dynamic, though, in *Caged Bird*, because of the string of wild-speaking characters like Sister Monroe and Mrs. Cullinan. Dialogue is far less frequent
as a stylistic device in more standard black autobiographies such as *The
Autobiography of Malcolm X* (1964) or Eldridge Cleaver's *Soul on Ice* (1968).

This same sentence, about the dentist's refusal to put his hand in
Maya's mouth, provides another example of metaphor. The discussion
of Maya's rape looks closely at the use of metaphor to communicate
overpowering pain. The reference to Negroes as dogs places Angelou's
use of metaphor within the stylistic tradition of black protest literature.
In much African American literature, one finds the theme of dehumanization, meaning the state of being denied human qualities such as intelligence, sensitivity, and so forth. Thus, the hero of Richard Wright's
The Man Who Lived Underground (1944) is depicted as less than human:
he crouches in a sewer and gnaws on a pork chop bone, as do dogs.
Claude McKay, in his poem "If We Must Die" (1919), uses a series of
animal references to convey the dehumanization of black men in America—hogs, barking dogs, and packs of doglike men—to emphasize the
ferocity of whites and the victimization of blacks.

There are a number of such references in *I Know Why the Caged Bird
Sings*. At the beginning of the book, Bailey and Maya wear instructions

on their wrists announcing their names and destination: like cattle, they are named and branded. Maya, who initially pities her mother's lonely boyfriend, compares him to some cute little pigs who were slaughtered in Stamps for sausage. After the trial, Grandmother Baxter calls Freeman a "mad dog" (72). These comparisons are precise, exact. In fact Angelou's most valued technique as a stylist may be the precision with which she describes objects or places, a precision so sharp that readers carry the descriptions with them, even when the book is closed. Her observations are sensual, keen to the essences of smell, sound, and sight. Her writing resembles a series of photographs or fragments of music: snapshots taken from many angles, notes played from a variety of instruments.

Although Sondra O'Neale (1984) claims that Angelou, for the most part, avoids a stereotypical black vocabulary and that her style reflects the rich language of her literary models (Poe, Dunbar, Dostoyevsky, to name a few), readers should have ears tuned to the folksy charm of *Caged Bird*, to Angelou's drawing on Southern speech patterns such as Momma's saying "didn't cotton to" (39) or "he gonna be that kind of nasty" (164). The narrator of *Caged Bird* projects a youthful exuberance as she harvests one figure of speech after another from her fertile imagination.

Reports from newspapers and Internet sources suggest that not all readers appreciate the effectiveness of Angelou's language. An Edgewater, Maryland mother has campaigned against *Caged Bird* being a required book in South River High School because it is "sexually explicit, racially divisive and too graphic about lesbianism" (Gross 1997, A1). In Mebane, North Carolina, in the state where Angelou now lives, writes, and teaches, similar charges were brought against her poetry. Threatened with losing his job for bringing Angelou's poetry to class, a fourth grade teacher apologized: "I never in my wildest dreams thought that anybody who would read a poem at the presidential inauguration could write such filth," he commented (http://www.blackvoices.com/thenews/97/).

Unhappily, this fear of Angelou's truth-telling has been spreading as white parents discover her power and confront the anger of *Caged Bird*, a black classic written nearly three decades ago. One news source, summarizing the censorship of *I Know Why the Caged Bird Sings*, claims that it was the book "most frequently challenged in schools in the 1995–1996 academic year" (http//www.planetout.com/pno/newsplanet/article.html/1998/01/13/4).

Parents' growing objections to *Caged Bird* lead to a final aspect of Angelou's style, one that distinguishes it from so many other autobiographies. That is its element of candor, of openness, as though she were telling the truth and nothing else—"as if" because Angelou the autobiographer sometimes changes the truth for artistic reasons, as in *Gather Together in My Name* (see Chapter 4). What matters from a literary standpoint is not the question of Angelou's telling the absolute truth but rather her gift of convincing readers of the narrator's desire to be accurate, so that her rape becomes a believable account of a young black girl's horrifying experience. Profanity and sexual references are a necessary part of this experience.

A FEMINIST READING

Feminism is a system of thought that is focused on women's rights. It insists on equality of women in the home, the marketplace, and in those institutions that control women's lives: education, medicine, government, and so on. One basic feminist assumption is that women are victims in a patriarchal society, in which power is held by the father or by his male representatives in the community, and in which all important decisions are made by men. Women who contest those decisions in the quest for social change are feminists, whether they identify with the term or not.

Most scholars trace the origins of feminism to the Industrial Revolution in Europe and America in the late-eighteenth and nineteenth centuries. As large groups of working men experienced democracy and freedom for the first time, women began to demand similar privileges— the right to vote, to own property, to control their bodies and their minds (Wright 1992, 98–99). In America, the feminist movement grew and then subsided in the 1920s, after women won the right to vote.

A second wave of feminism began to surge in America in 1970, the year *Caged Bird* was published. Called the New Women's Movement, this revival of feminism was indebted to the civil-rights movement of the 1960s, with its grassroots appeal and its strategies for social change. After a number of black women refused to accept inferior positions in the Student Nonviolent Coordinating Committee (SNCC) and the Congress of Racial Equality (CORE) the two leading civil rights groups, a split occurred along gender lines. Many black women separated themselves from male authority and formed their own organizations on campuses and in the community.

The heroine of *Caged Bird* arrived on the literary scene in 1970, at the very moment when women in America were creating black sister's leagues or forming small discussion groups to share their experiences of oppression under the patriarchal order. A year before the publication of *Caged Bird*, black poet Sonia Sanchez introduced a course, "The Black Woman," at the University of Pittsburgh, the first college course to concentrate on the experiences of black women in the Americas (Tierney 1989, 45). Emerging American feminists were getting ready to learn, to discuss, to listen. The time was ripe for *I Know Why the Caged Bird Sings*.

Angelou herself worked with pro-African women's groups through her affiliation with the Cultural Association for Women of African Heritage (CAWAH). The women of CAWAH organized a sit-in at the United Nations Building in New York after Patrice Lumumba, the prime minister of Zaire, was assassinated. Angelou also accepted a leadership role in the civil-rights movement after Martin Luther King Jr. invited her to become Northern Coordinator of the Southern Christian Leadership Conference (SCLC). It is unlikely that she affiliated with groups exclusively defined as feminist. When asked if she is a feminist or if she supports the feminist cause, Angelou has been vague. She told Jeffrey M. Elliot that she considers black women to be more self-reliant than white women. She also believes in "equal pay, equal respect, equal responsibility" for everyone (1989, 93). As for her being a feminist, Angelou has a practical but elusive comment: "I am a feminist. I've been female for a long time now. I'd be stupid not to be on my own side" (Forma, qtd. in Elliot 1989, 162).

A feminist reading of *I Know Why the Caged Bird Sings* raises a number of questions relating to women and their social conditions. First, does *Caged Bird* develop themes of specific relevance to women? Second, is *Caged Bird* centered around a strong, aware female character or characters? Third, do the women characters bond with other women in an effort to change conditions under the patriarchy?

The first question, is *Caged Bird*'s theme relevant to women? is emphatically answered in the text. Momma Henderson's nurturing of her granddaughter mirrors the mother/daughter relationship that forms the emotional foundation of feminism. As Marianne Hirsch argues, feminists must "find ways to speak as mothers" if they ever hope to estimate and understand women's differences (1989, 195). Maya is daughter, granddaughter, and finally mother as she charts her development as a woman. She is concerned with the women in her community, even though she sometimes sees their lives as limited. Like the majority of women, she gives birth to a child. Because the various plot strands in *Caged Bird* are tied to the theme of motherhood, it is an excellent example of a feminist book.

With regard to the second question, the central female character of *Caged Bird* does not project a strong, positive image of women. In one of the most quoted phrases from the book she describes herself as an "ugly black dream" (2). Unfortunately, Maya shows contempt for herself in the parts of the autobiography that take place in Stamps and St. Louis, for reasons that have to do with her racial and sexual attitudes.

When she is raped by Mr. Freeman, Maya's self-esteem plunges to the point where she refuses to speak. Not until she regains her voice and moves to California does her sense of self-worth expand. Although Maya is to some degree a negative character, she is a potential feminist because she is aware of the forces in society that are working against her.

In answer to the third question, does the character in the autobiography form bonding relationships with other women? Maya does bond with other women on a close, personal level, but she and the other women of Stamps are unable to affect any major changes in the patriarchy. Black women in the later 1930s, although they could influence each other's lives, had no power to question the social order because the people in power were white and racist. There were no civil-rights laws to protect political dissenters in Arkansas. Were a woman to challenge the system in Stamps, Arkansas, in the 1930s or 1940s or in the decades to come, she ended up dead. Only years later, when Maya leaves Stamps and goes to California, does she challenge the patriarchal order by becoming the first black female streetcar conductor in San Francisco.

On a personal level, there are significant bonding relationships among women. The bonding that takes place between Maya and Mrs. Flowers clearly supports the reading of *Caged Bird* as a model for feminist autobiography. Mrs. Flowers is the primary example of feminism in Stamps: She is independent, she has the economic resources to survive on her own; she respects herself; and she cares about other women, to the extent that she takes control of Maya's education, helping her to read and regain her own voice. Without her, Maya would never have become a writer.

At the end of the narrative, Maya returns to her mother, Vivian Baxter—city woman, blackjack dealer, and free spirit. She is able to draw from Vivian Baxter the strength and support she needs as she prepares to have a baby. Thus, *I Know Why the Caged Bird Sings*, which begins with the separation of mother and daughter, ends in their bonding. The mother/daughter/infant triangle of the final scene marks the completion of Maya's journey to womanhood. Although she is still fearful and dependent, she shows signs of being able to control her life as a black woman.

Gather Together in My Name
(1974)

Gather Together in My Name begins in San Francisco shortly after the end of the Second World War. The illusion of racial equality in San Francisco during the war years begins to vanish. With white soldiers reclaiming their lives as civilians, black workers were expected to return to their farms and black military heroes to their ghettos. Angelou's prefatory observations about race and the job market are intended to place the autobiographer within an historic framework, with her personal economic situation echoing the postwar decline of African American society.

At seventeen, Maya is looking for a job that will bring her recognition, money, and independence, but she lacks the skills necessary to achieve these goals in a dominant white economy. Additionally, she believes, as do many young women, that to achieve her own goals she must leave her mother and stepfather, who have supported her, and define a new life for herself and for her two-month-old son. Leaving her family thus creates a double bind for the struggling single mother; she depends on them, but at the same time she wants to be independent.

Gather Together traces Maya's emergence into the world of work, carefully recounting her pursuit of economic stability as she moves from job to job—from Creole cook, to dancer, to prostitute, to fry cook. During the course of the autobiography she sometimes acts irresponsibly, when she endangers the safety of her son who is kidnapped by a baby-sitter.

She also exposes herself to a number of risky relationships with men: a dancer; a married man who sells stolen clothes; a vein-scarred drug user.

At the end of *Gather Together*, she is finally saved when her most reliable friend, Troubador Martin, demonstrates the dangers of drug addiction by walking her through a heroin den. Shocked and repentant, Angelou, in a promise to reclaim her innocence, abandons her degenerate life and vows to return with her son to her mother's protection.

NARRATIVE POINT OF VIEW

In *Gather Together in My Name*, Angelou continues but alters the point of view of *Caged Bird*. *Caged Bird* is the first-person account of a child who becomes a mother; *Gather Together* is the first-person account of that mother and her struggle to survive as a black woman in white America. Thus, the autobiographical form makes a surprising leap away from the growing pains of the sensitive child narrator of *I Know Why the Caged Bird Sings* to the survival tactics of the continuation of the narrative. Despite the difference, Angelou continues, as in *Caged Bird*, to challenge the norm of standard American autobiographies, in which the narrator is usually a prominent, educated white male.

The Maya of *Caged Bird* is easily recognizable as a child growing up in rural America whose experiences of abandonment and rape make her as memorable, in her way, as Mark Twain's adventuresome Huckleberry Finn is memorable in his way. The Maya of *Gather Together* is a different kind of woman, a Maya who has come of age, a survivor whose endurance is representative of a new class of black women. The point of view thus changes from that of an engaging girl to a sexy, willful mother who is the same person but dramatically different. Angelou's unorthodox altering of the growing-up pattern or *Bildungsroman* by way of a sequel surprised her critics, many of whom never guessed that the author would transform the girl from Stamps into the loose-living mother from California.

Angelou's deviation from proper conduct was a violation of autobiographical tradition. A black woman who deals with lesbians, hookers, and drug addicts, is bound to rock the standards used for centuries in evaluating American and European autobiography. Traditionally, the genre has been subdivided into professions occupied by men: statesmen, educators, soldiers, financiers, church fathers, and the like. Not until the civil-rights and women's movements of the 1960s and 1970s did a significant number of writers challenge this elitist notion of life telling. Like Ann Moody's *Coming of Age in Mississippi* (1968) and Eldridge Cleaver's *Soul on Ice* (1968), *Gather Together in My Name* is one of several contemporary black texts that reinvent the very notion of autobiographical decorum. They tell it like it is, without obeying the strictures of language and behavior found in mainstream works.

When she first tries to tell her story, Angelou confessed to her difficulty with point of view. She felt that she was fragmented, that to convey her personality she would have to split herself into two women, one respectable and the other improper, one the autobiographer and the other her seamier self. "I wanted this fictional girl to do all the bad things and I was Miss Goodie Two Shoes," she explained in an interview. She thought she needed to have "a fictional character go along side, I guess in the margins." She told her editor, Bob Loomis, about the plan and he said, "Try it." But it didn't work. So her husband Paul encouraged her to reject this split point of view, believing that the truth of her experience was real and whole: "Tell it. Because if it happened to black girls it happened to black boys, happened to white girls it happened to white boys. This is true" ("Icon" 1997).

Angelou told this writer that before *Gather Together* was published, she became increasingly worried about the adverse effect her autobiographical truth saying might have on her family. Thus, she gathered them together—Bailey, Vivian Baxter, her husband Paul Du Feu, and Guy, the name used throughout this companion for her son—and read to them the sections on prostitution and drugs. And she said, "I want to read you this. If it hurts you, I won't put it in." Each accepted what she had written about her life—Vivian with a joke, Bailey with absolute trust. "My brother said, 'I love you. One thing about you, you don't lie. I love that.'" As for Guy, Angelou continued, "He came between me and my husband and just took me and said, 'You are the great one'" ("Icon" 1997). Her family's encouragement made it possible for her to represent a young black woman's struggle tell the truth, even when the truth could possibly cause harm to herself and others.

Like the literary titles of the other four autobiographies, the title *Gather Together in My Name* is elusive, perplexing. It seems to relate, as Sondra O'Neale argues, to a New Testament passage that calls the "travailing soul to pray and commune" (1984, 33). Although Angelou does not discourage a religious reading, she offers a more specific interpretation, explaining that too many parents lie to their children about the past. She says: "Somebody needs to tell young people, listen, I did this and I did that. I thought, all those parents who lie, and fudge, and evade and avoid, could gather together in my name and I would say it" ("Icon" 1997).

Angelou wanted the title, *Gather Together in My Name*, to convey the same point of view inherent in the autobiography—the narrator wanted her gathering of readers to know what had happened to her so that other young people in similar straits could avoid the same pitfalls. It seems, then, that the narrator of Angelou's most controversial book is gathering a double audience: young people who need direction and older people who need to give it. In her name the tarnished past will come forth. The truth will be told.

What the narrator achieves in the second volume is a remarkable sense of authenticity. As a straightforward recorder of life, she replaces the smooth chronology of *Caged Bird* for an episodic series of fragments that mirror the kind of discord found in actual life. *Gather Together* has an expanded consciousness that enables the reader to identify with an African American woman experiencing life among a diverse class of people including prostitutes. Sondra O'Neale writes that Angelou "so painstakingly details the girl's descent into the brothel that Black women, all women, have enough vicarious example to avoid the trap" (1984, 32).

At least one black woman experiences the kind of salvation that O'Neale is describing. A young woman came to a book signing in Cleveland, Ohio, shortly after *Gather Together* was published. It was a large crowd, and Angelou tried to speak to everyone in turn: "Suddenly there was this girl, black girl, with false nails, badly put on, and I looked up, and she had fake hair hanging down, false eyelashes, and it was 10:30, 11:00 in the morning. In a micro-miniskirt. I said, 'Hello. And your name?' She leaned over and she said, 'I saw you on television. You even give me hope.'" Angelou paused. "If she's the only person I wrote the book for, it's all right, because I talked to her" ("Icon" 1997).

As it turns out, the girl in the miniskirt is not the only person Angelou wrote the book for. Despite some negative reviews, and despite some rather unflattering remarks from one television commentator, the Maya of *Gather Together in My Name* is an inspiring woman primarily because of what she dares to reveal about herself. Her point of view in this second volume can best be described as open or naked—a first-person perspective so honest that autobiography becomes personal contact.

STRUCTURE

Each of Angelou's autobiographies is structured through the use of a journey, either an extensive one such as from America to Europe in *Singin' and Swingin' and Gettin' Merry Like Christmas* (1976), or a condensed one, as in the San Francisco-Stamps-St. Louis triad in *Caged Bird*. In contrast, the movement in *Gather Together* consists of far smaller segments or episodes, almost like bus rides or, to use a more artistic comparison, like dance movements. Thus, Angelou recounts her work and sexual experiences in a rhythm familiar to the many young black people who, like her, have been excluded from high-paying careers or elegant housing. She circles in place, at the edge of the dance floor, whereas in the following three volumes she is in the air, like a bird or a jet, soaring to Europe, Africa, Germany, and back to Africa.

Like certain kinds of twentieth-century African American music, especially jazz, *Gather Together in My Name* has a musical structure in which several melodies are played simultaneously by different instruments. These melodies intertwine or cross each other. For example, the piano and the saxophone play against each other in John Coltrane's monumental album *My Favorite Things*, recorded in the early 1960s around the time when Angelou was in Ghana. This crossing of sounds, called "polyphony," rarely results in harmony.

Like the masters of modern jazz, Angelou structures *Gather Together* by recalling a series of discordant episodes or chords, scenes so dissimilar in texture that they give the autobiography a chaotic or fragmented quality. For example, when Maya finally gets to dance, she feels eternally anchored to the spot, as if a "stake had been driven down through my head and body" (102). In the next episode, without a transition, Maya visits her mother, who is cooking dinner for a male friend. Maya agrees to run to the neighborhood grocery store, only to discover on her return that Vivian has stabbed David, one of her lovers, who attacked Vivian for inviting a rival for dinner. The layering of images—dancing and eating, the stake and the knife, lover A, lover B—creates the impression of upheaval. The two episodes immediately follow one another, like a double exposure or two pieces of cellophane stuck together. Although Maya is the ordering element—the thread through the text—she experiences such a variety of disjointed incidents that at first there seems to be little connection among them. This layering of narrative elements resembles polyphony and creates the kind of ordered chaos that characterizes Angelou's style, and themes.

In gathering together the disparate episodes into a loosely rounded structure, Angelou initiates what Dolly A. McPherson calls "the pattern of a circuitous journey" (1990, 70). The journey in the second volume resembles a choppy tour through the coarser side of San Francisco and its surrounding communities. These wanderings are interrupted by two journeys outside the city: to Stamps, Arkansas, to visit Annie Henderson, and to Bakersfield, California, to rescue her kidnapped son from the baby-sitter known as Big Mary.

PLOT DEVELOPMENT

In autobiography, plot usually provides a chronological overview of the actions relayed in the story. According to Meyer H. Abrams, a unified plot is one that has a "complete and ordered structure of actions" (1993, 160). Such a definition does not seem relevant to *Gather Together*, in that the actions seem unstructured and the narrative incomplete.

The plot of *Gather Together* is concerned with a young black woman who describes in detail the process of becoming an adult, emphasizing parenting, personal development, and survival. Survival, in Angelou's case, is defined as her perseverance in dealing with the emotional, racial, economic, and relational aspects of her life. Her apprehensions about her son, coupled with her recurring sense of being an inadequate mother, create a special kind of tension, repeated and interconnected as the plot is relocated from one autobiography to the next.

The plot resembles a walk through the underworld, with Angelou's salvation at the end hoped for but in no way guaranteed. She is still a girl, unfinished, like autobiography itself. In the process of becoming, the narrator, like the plot, is "open-ended and incomplete . . . always in process" (Olney 1980, 25).

Gather Together stands out from Angelou's other autobiographies because it is the one in which the details of plot are centered almost exclusively in one geographical area, the city of San Francisco, California. Ironically, the concentrated locale produces the most disjointed of Angelou's plots; she lacks the necessary power over events and now the plot is in control, squeezing her into the unpleasant situations that are her life. Without money, without support from friends, she has no place to run to, no way to propel herself into the sweeping spaces of her later volumes.

Another important plot distinction is that the second volume initiates the series. No longer does *I Know Why the Caged Bird Sings* stand alone as a single-volume autobiography. Unwilling to let this very successful first volume be her last word, Angelou deviates from the conventional plot by continuing her life story in a second volume. The ending of *Caged Bird* is no longer the "complete and ordered structure of actions" defined by Abrams. Rather, it is the catalyst for a new beginning.

CHARACTER DEVELOPMENT

Angelou begins the story of *Gather Together* with a blunt, factual state-ment about her character: "I was seventeen, very old, embarrassingly young, with a son of two months, and I still lived with my mother and stepfather" (3). She is in conflict between being too old and too young, too responsible (she has a son) but too dependent (she lives at home). Maya's character develops, as it does to some extent in all of the vol-umes, through this sort of opposition.

Like the fluctuating plot of *Gather Together*, the character of its narrator shifts and flickers. Maya is never firmly grounded, always changing jobs, lovers, perspectives. Her life is irritating, often painful. In an interview she remarked that in *Gather Together* she "wrote about the unpleasant, well not just unpleasant, but the certain parts of our lives that are very painful" ("Icon" 1997). Her pain and dislocation are, once again, alien to the spirit of more optimistic autobiographical accounts like Zora Neale Hurston's *Dust Tracks on a Road* (1942) or Nikki Giovanni's *Gemini* (1971) or Angelou's own *Caged Bird*. What happened, readers wondered, to the sprightly, imaginative child who lived in Arkansas?

In 1974, when Random House published *Gather Together*, respected critics were disappointed with Angelou's changed character. Selwyn R. Cudjoe claimed that *Caged Bird* had a stable "moral center," but *Gather Together* was fragmented, therefore "weak." He particularly objected to the sequel's sense of "alienation and fragmentation" (1984, 17). Like Cudjoe, Lynn Z. Bloom found the second volume disappointing; she felt that *Gather Together* lacked the "maturity, honesty, and intuitive good judgment" of *Caged Bird* (1985, 5).

Yet if looked at carefully, it becomes obvious that Maya in *Gather To-*

gether is not terribly different from the Maya in *Caged Bird*. The dance-obsessed mother of the second volume is merely an extension of the adventuresome heroine of *I Know Why the Caged Bird Sings*—not the preteen who quietly reads Shakespeare, but the wild child who deliberately gets herself pregnant and who, without knowing how to drive, steers a car down a mountainside in Mexico while her drunk father sleeps in the passenger seat. Critics paid little attention to the summer vacation in southern California with Bailey Sr. and his knife-swinging girlfriend, Dolores. Yet in that episode, which covers twenty-six pages of text, Angelou predicts the person she becomes in *Gather Together*: rebellious, risk-taking, reckless, audacious.

What is more, Cudjoe, Bloom, and other critics tend to overlook the strength of character that make *Gather Together* so convincing an autobiography and Maya so captivating a narrator. Dolly A. McPherson argues that the fragmentation of character and plot in *Gather Together in My Name* is a merit rather than a flaw, since it artistically reflects the "alienated fragmented nature of Angelou's life" (1990, 62–63). The word "fragmentation" is used in this context to convey a sense of incompleteness or disconnection.

Maya's fragmentation can be observed in any number of her relationships: with her mother, with the women she tries to control, with her grandmother, with her lovers. Vivian Baxter, the absent mother of *Caged Bird*, is restored to importance in the second volume. *Gather Together* begins and ends with Maya's mother. At the start, Maya and her child are living with Vivian and Daddy Clidell, Maya's stepfather. As a matter of pride, Maya decides to leave and get a job, taking her son Guy with her. When the book ends, Maya and Guy intend to return to the protection of Vivian Baxter, following Angelou's glimpse at the horrors of heroin addiction. In its promised reunion of mother, child, and grandmother, the concluding paragraph directly parallels the ending of *Caged Bird*: Vivian turns out the lights of her house as Maya and her baby fall asleep.

Fragmentation is also a component of her relationships with other women. In *Caged Bird* Maya has one girlfriend, Louise Kendricks. A lonely girl, Louise has the kind of imagination that appealed to Maya. They hold hands, close their eyes, and pretend to be dropping from the sky. Together Maya and Louise "challenge the unknown" (119). The suggestive description of Louise, along with Maya's concern about being a lesbian, takes a much sharper focus in *Gather Together*. Here there is no sweet Louise. Maya becomes a madam and the women who work for her, Beatrice and Johnnie Mae, are lesbians and prostitutes. The relationships between Maya and her whores are fragmented, built on distrust, controlled by Maya's desire for money.

Maya is quite aggressive in securing the services of Beatrice and Johnnie Mae. She promotes herself as a madam and persuades the lesbian couple to work as prostitutes in their own small home. Maya does well enough to buy a car and some clothes, but the arrangement disintegrates when Maya arrives late one night and finds the girls working after hours, in flagrant violation of Maya's orders. Johnnie Mae threatens to turn Maya over to the police, where she will be jailed for owning an automobile purchased with money earned illegally.

Following the shakedown with Johnnie Mae and Beatrice, Maya gathers Guy and her suitcase, abandons her car at the train station, and goes by rail to Stamps, in search of the "protective embrace" of Momma Henderson (61). For a while she works at Momma's store, although customers are constantly wondering why any woman who left for San Francisco would come back to Stamps. She gets drunk at the Dew Drop Inn with her high school friends. Guy is happy to receive the attention of Momma and Uncle Willie.

During her stay, Maya goes into the white area of town to purchase a Simplicity sewing pattern at the Stamps General Merchandise Store, only to find that the pattern has to be special ordered. The day she returns to pick it up is a hot, hot Southern day, so hot that Maya's "thighs scudded like wet rubber" (75). At the store she gets into trouble for talking brazenly to a saleswoman who has blocked her entry. Maya realizes that she has become too racially liberated to accept the restrictions of the white community. In a parallel manner, Momma Henderson has remained fearful of white intolerance and continues to adhere to the unspoken rules concerning whites. In a memorable scene, Momma slaps her rebellious grandchild again and again, ordering her to leave Stamps for her own protection and the baby's. It is the last moment of contact between them.

Although Maya's outspoken attitudes lead to a termination of their relationship, her grandmother continues to be a reminder of morality and Christian values. In San Francisco, one evening, Maya, now working as a prostitute, notices a cook on the premises, a woman who so reminds her of Annie Henderson that she has to lower her gaze when the servant puts dinner on the table. The cook in the whorehouse represents Momma

Henderson's continuing spiritual influence and reminds the reader of how far Maya has strayed from the teachings of the Christian Methodist Episcopal Church of Stamps, Arkansas.

Perhaps Maya's major source of fragmentation comes from her relationships with men. Priscilla R. Ramsey concludes that Angelou often misinterprets the behavior of men with whom she is infatuated. Because she becomes involved too quickly, she is "repeatedly hurt by men who are far more experienced than she, who are far more able to see her neediness and exploit it before she is able to see it in herself" (1984–85, 149).

Angelou's male companions are rarely constructive. While the adult males in *Caged Bird* are crippled, absent, or abusive, the men in *Gather Together* are manipulative, unfaithful, or damaged. Early in the second autobiography Maya meets Curly, who gives her her first "love party" (18). Overjoyed with the lovemaking, Maya senses maturity and pleasure for the first time. They take Guy to parks and playgrounds. Maya buys Curly an expensive ring on Daddy Clidell's charge account. Then one night he tells her that his girlfriend has come back from San Diego where she had been working in a shipyard.

In her distress over losing Curly, Maya turns to her brother, who is again her defender, as he had been in *Caged Bird*. Bailey works for decent pay on an ammunition boat out of San Diego. Promising her two hundred dollars, he persuades her to leave San Francisco and make a new start in San Diego. Meanwhile, Bailey marries a high-school chum named Eunice who, much to his despair, contracts tuberculosis and dies. Fragmented and incomplete after her death, Bailey has a breakdown, then turns to drugs to ease the emptiness.

Of the men who take advantage of Maya, L. D. Tolbrook is the worst. A married man, he lures Maya into becoming a prostitute for his sake. Professing that he owes money to some hardened criminals, Tolbrook convinces the "innocent" Maya to turn tricks. Perhaps the most interesting aspect of the whorehouse scenes is the dialogue. Maya's coworkers are intelligent women who know the trade. Clara, Maya's boss, advises further on how to talk and act when she's with a man. Clara promises that if she's good, L. D. (Daddy) will get her a "little white girl," meaning cocaine. Maya is beginning to suspect, from the way the whores talk, that Daddy is really a pimp, someone who is hiring her out for his own profit. When Maya tells Bailey how she is earning a living, he is furious. Once again Maya's savior, Bailey forces her to quit the whorehouse and orders her to warn Tolbrook that her brother Bailey is after him.

The climax of *Gather Together in My Name* occurs when an unexpectedly compassionate boyfriend, Troubador Martin, takes Maya, now smoking a lot of marijuana, on an unnerving tour of the underworld of heroin addiction. Troub makes her watch while he shoots up, makes her watch as the needle punctures a scab and "rich yellow pus" runs down his arm (180). Maya's refusal, at Troub's advice, to do hard drugs marks the end of her irresponsibility and the inauguration of new standards that help safeguard her and her son's survival.

The end of *Gather Together* gives little indication that someday Maya will be a successful performer, wife, or mother. Deserted by her dancing partner, R. L. Poole, and betrayed by her pimp, L. D. Tolbrook, the best break she receives by the end of the narrative is to have narrowly escaped heroin addiction. The book closes with an experienced Maya preparing to return to her mother's protection: "I had no idea what I was going to make of my life, but I had given a promise and found my innocence. I swore I'd never lose it again" (181).

Although the reader may feel jolted by the suddenness of the ending, this sort of high-speed projection into the future is a common element in Angelou's conclusions. Sondra O'Neale comments on the "abrupt suspense" and drama with which the central character draws together her story: "In this way dramatic technique not only centralizes each work, it also makes the series narrative a collective whole" (1984, 33).

The Maya of *Gather Together in My Name* is a person of potential strength and moral integrity, perhaps even "innocence," who is struggling against the temptations that the fast world of California is holding before her: sex, money, getting high. Through it all, the narrator is determined to present Maya as honestly as possible, in a way that readers will believe: "Young people feel safe with me," she claims, "because they know I'm not going to lie and I won't fudge. I'm not going to tell them everything I know, but I will try to make sure that what I say is the truth" ("Icon" 1997).

SETTING

With the exception of a return visit to Stamps, the setting in *Gather Together* is confined to the state of California. The setting includes the various dwellings where Maya and her son are forced to live, sometimes separately; the job sites where she feels threatened or demeaned; the places that offer her temporary contentment, like Vivian's house in San Francisco and Annie Henderson's store in Stamps, Arkansas.

The narrative opens in a smooth and leisurely manner, at the San Francisco residence of Vivian Baxter and Daddy Clidell. When Maya leaves on her quest for independence, the setting changes swiftly: one day she works in a hospital cafeteria, the next as a cook in a Creole restaurant. She moves from San Francisco to Los Angeles, to San Diego then Stockton, and back, trying to provide for her son. Always in motion, always changing, Maya circles her surroundings as she looks for work, for love, for contentment.

The dizzy changes of setting culminate when Maya, fearing that Johnnie Mae will report her for having an illegal automobile, goes with Guy to Stamps on a desperate train ride that echoes the two children with name tags at the beginning of *I Know Why the Caged Bird Sings*. In the first volume, the small town in Arkansas represents a state of innocence, a place of refuge for two lonely and unwanted children. In *Gather Together*, Stamps cannot offer solace to Maya, whose knowledge of city life makes her challenge Momma Henderson's unbending rule that you just don't talk to white folks. When Maya, in violation of her grandmother's wishes, leaves the black community of Stamps and crosses the dusty road into the white section of Stamps, she initiates a confrontation with two white saleswomen that Momma Henderson hears about even before Maya gets back to the store. Maya's violation of decorum results in a severe beating from Momma and a prompt return to California.

THEMATIC ISSUES

In creating an autobiography, the narrator depends on thematic issues to act as reflections on character and plot. A theme is a repeated motif that creates a pattern or design in the text. When it is skillfully handled, as it is in *Gather Together*, theme can enrich the plot, help organize the volume, and even determine how the plot begins and ends. Three major themes dominate *Gather Together*—motherhood, clothing, and work.

The theme of motherhood controls the plot of *Gather Together*. Maya makes decisions or forms relationships with the constant image of her son before her, as she tries to provide him with a stable environment or console herself when they are separated. Maya's motherhood is what keeps her connected to the world of responsibility. However, she often falls short in her duties as mother, due to complications in her work or the enticements of her male friends, who also want time with her. This situation highlights the duality Maya feels throughout the series between mothering and working.

Recall the mother/mother/son still life—Vivian, Maya, and the baby in repose—with which Angelou ended *I Know Why the Caged Bird Sings*. This tranquil scene is disrupted in *Gather Together* as the young mother roams the streets of San Francisco looking for a way to survive. In the second volume she inverts the motherhood theme of *Caged Bird*: the little girl who longed for Vivian's love is now a mother herself, a teenage girl responsible for the nurturing of her son. In so doing, Maya's mother in *Gather Together* replaces Maya as daughter in *Caged Bird* and the theme of motherhood is at the center of the rest of the autobiographies in the series.

With the theme of motherhood Angelou engages the reader in a mother/child configuration that is of vital concern for the remaining autobiographies. As Marianne Hirsch argues in another context, African American women writers during the last three decades are one of the few groups who tell the mother's story and feature the mother in "complex and multiple ways" (1990, 414). In developing the theme of motherhood, Angelou applies the same quality of honesty to her role of mother as she does to her role of prostitute; in fact, the two tend to interconnect in their elements of pain, struggle, imperfection, and loss.

One of the problems any working mother faces is finding child care. Maya needs an adequate sitter to care for Guy while she is working, which means, at least in the case of being a prostitute, all-night assistance. She finds an excellent sitter in Mother Cleo, a fat woman who likes babies and even takes in white infants, although she charges more for them. Another sitter, acquired after the interlude in Stamps, is Big Mary Dalton an affectionate woman who lives in Stockton, where Maya takes a job first as a fry cook and then as a prostitute. Big Mary arranges for Guy to live in her house, with Maya taking her son on her day off. After she meets L. D. Tolbrook, though, Maya occasionally forfeits her day off with Guy to be with her boyfriend.

In a powerful treatment of child loss in *Gather Together in My Name*, Maya goes to Big Mary's house and finds it deserted. A neighbor tells her that Big Mary moved away three days earlier and that she probably

went to her brother's in Bakersfield. After a desperate search and a long
bus ride, Maya locates Big Mary Dalton and her angry son, whose feelings of abandonment echo her own unhappiness during childhood.

Of the numerous references in *Gather Together* that address Maya's
feelings of inadequacy as a mother, the Big Mary episode is surely one.
Guy cries, pulls his mother's hair, and expresses his fury at being deserted for so long a time. Maya sheds bitter tears and acknowledges her
"first guilt" (163). Earlier in the autobiography Maya admits to having
ignored her son to such an extent that Big Mary Dalton asked: "Ain't
you got time for him?" (147). She also leaves him alone on the night that
Troubadour Martin ushers her to the drug den near the San Francisco
docks. These and other instances of maternal conflict or neglect give
Gather Together a special tension. The tension does not vanish in the volume's affirmation of "innocence" but continues with lesser or greater
gravity throughout the series.

The second theme, clothing, is also of great importance in the writings
of African American women. Clothing is an indicator of class and character; black women writers often use clothing symbolically, as a kind of
second skin or mask. In Paule Marshall's *Praisesong for the Widow* (1984),
for example, the heroine is on a cruise ship. The six suitcases filled with
linen dresses and evening gowns become, on both literal and symbolic
levels, the excess baggage that keeps her trapped in bourgeois values.
Similarly, Jade, the light-skinned model in Toni Morrison's *Tar Baby*
(1981), owns a sealskin coat, a rich, black fur that covers her sleek body.
The coat becomes a multileveled symbol in the novel—a barricade between her and her primitive lover; a sign of capitalism, with its slaughter
of innocent seals for profit; a reference to the famed tar baby of African
American folklore that traps its victims and won't let go.

Angelou introduces clothing as a theme on the first page of *I Know
Why the Caged Bird Sings*. Her ugly purple frock made a noise "like crepe
paper on the back of hearse." A sign of her humiliation, the dress is also,
as Liliane K. Arensberg (1976) observes, symbolic of the themes of death
and rebirth that operate in the first autobiography. In *Gather Together in
My Name*, however, the clothing theme is less austere. Here Angelou
tends to use clothing as a form of deliberate costuming that either covers
up or augments her character's body, often conveying her bad taste and
inexperience. Frequently, the way she dresses is determined by the men
she is involved with.

Similarly, the theme of clothing is also introduced on the first page of
Gather Together, in a description of San Francisco during the Second

World War. Black women from the South, who knew only "maid's uniforms and mammy-made dresses," changed these garments for men's work pants and took jobs in the shipyards. Prostitutes were so busy they didn't have time to take off their shoes, the narrator remarks in the prologue, foreshadowing Maya's later work as a prostitute and madam.

Clothes become a tool of the trade when L. D. Tolbrook begs her to "dress her age" in short skirts, ankle socks, and hair ribbons. Teenage attire becomes her identifying feature as a prostitute and her clothing an ironic statement about the theme of innocence that helps structure the book. At the end of the autobiography, Maya regains her "innocence," lost through her use of drugs, prostitution, and subservience to men and their fantasies. Other references to clothes also point out the incongruity of her "innocence," for instance when Troubador Martin stashes stolen clothing in her rooms until Maya's closets are stuffed with sweaters and skirts; or her buying a too revealing dance costume for her first Poole and Rita performance.

Clothing takes on special significance when she returns to Stamps wearing her city clothing: white, off-the-shoulder peasant blouses and brightly colored skirts with floral prints. Her high-school friend, L. C. Smith, tells Maya the truth. Everyone is laughing at her for wearing "the very clothes everyone here wants to get rid of" (69). Maya's reason for going to the white section of Stamps is presumably to change her manner of dress, for she orders a Simplicity sewing pattern for a design not available in Stamps. Reading the situation symbolically, Simplicity can be associated with innocence. The specific pattern, too complicated for the Stamps General Merchandise Store to stock, marks the end of Maya's simplistic and innocent life in Stamps. Because of her arrogant outburst over a piece of clothing that doesn't exist, Maya and Guy are finished in Stamps, ordered away for their own good by Annie Henderson.

A third theme, work, is also connected to related ideas in each of the volumes. Recall Maya's delight in *Caged Bird* at being hired as the first black streetcar conductor in San Francisco. In *Gather Together*, work is of supreme importance as the narrator persistently searches for a means of survival. Her greatest job disappointment occurs when, about to be inducted as an army recruit, Maya is suddenly rejected because the army learns that she attended the Mission Labor School for two years, a school on the list of the House Un-American Activities Committee. HUAC, a committee created by the authority of the United States Senate, was headed by Senator Joseph McCarthy (1908–1957). Its business was to uncover Communists among educators, entertainers, governmental employees, the Army, the State Department, and anywhere else sus-pected of sheltering "Reds" or "Commies." The army says "No," even though they have no evidence that Maya was ever a communist sym-pathizer.

She is more fortunate with other job applications in service or enter-tainment businesses: cafeteria worker, cook, prostitute, dancer, and so forth. Food service—short-order cook, waitress, restaurant manager—offers work that Maya feels fairly comfortable with, perhaps because of Annie Henderson's great success in selling lunches to mill workers in Arkansas during the depression. Although Maya's work in a San Fran-cisco diner is very depressing, she lifts her spirits by listening to jazz: "I let the music wash away the odors and moods of the restaurant" (80). Her restaurant jobs eventually become ways to meet male friends, who, like her jobs, tend to be short-term and unreliable.

Maya loses one decent job as the manager of a small restaurant in Oakland because of her own compassionate personality. Appalled to dis-cover that her boss, Mr. Cain, promotes prizefighting, she becomes hys-terical when she sees a small young boxer who looks like Bailey being "whooped" to death. When Maya starts screaming "Stop them" and "Freak," she knows her job is over (173–74).

A second category of work in *Gather Together*, and one that has the greatest impact on her later years, involves the entertainment industry. As an individual or as part of a team, Maya shows promise as a dancer and cabaret singer. In a display of modesty, though, she refuses to dance nude for stag parties, telling R. L. Poole that she won't have a "bunch of white men to gape at me" (113). Maya learns her routines quickly and incorporates the steps into the Poole and Rita reviews until Poole's girl-friend returns to replace Maya as his partner. By the time of the third volume, *Singin' and Swingin' and Gettin' Merry Like Christmas* (1976), Maya's talent and diligence earns her a solid reputation as a performer, solid enough to be offered the opportunity to dance in George Gersh-win's *Porgy and Bess*.

A third kind of work in *Gather Together* involves illicit sex. One night in a bar where Maya works as a B-girl, pushing watered-down drinks at inflated prices, she meets two lesbians, Beatrice and Johnnie Mae. As usual, she is suspicious of gay women. Nevertheless, she accepts an in-vitation to visit them at their house, where she smokes marijuana for the first time and where, maybe because she's high, she concocts a plan to be their business manager or madam while Johnnie Mae and Beatrice turn tricks. In this capacity she makes enough money to buy a car.

While the idea of being a prostitute disgusts Maya at first, she later succumbs to the wishes of L. D. Tolbrook, who begs her to prostitute herself for him so that he can pay off his debts. Maya is the least popular of the three whores at Clara's. As Clara warns her, men don't want to get married, they just want to "trick" (141). Maya dislikes the strong smell of disinfectant but enjoys the way the women talk to each other. The whorehouse scenes contain exactly the kind of material that Angelou was afraid to disclose to the public, fearing that her family would be offended if they knew she had been a prostitute. Nonetheless, the theme of sexuality in *Gather Together* reveals a great deal of honesty and daring on the part of the narrator.

STYLE AND LITERARY DEVICES

Due to the provocative sexual nature of *Gather Together*, Angelou's writing in this volume is a mixture of elegant, mature prose coupled with the language of low-life characters for whom "reefer," "trick," and "pimp" are major words in their vocabularies. At times, Angelou seems to sink along with her troubles to the very depths of the earth; she describes the "slimy world" of prostitution with a sensuousness that exudes the feel of a "man's zipper" on her thigh, the feel of Lysol irritating her throat (140–41). Even when she writes with eloquence, her topics tend to be grim, as in her description of Bailey following the death of his wife from tuberculosis, or in her presentation of her breakup with Curly.

Only rarely is an elated Maya stretching her wings. She is most ecstatic when she is onstage, with the movement of the dance pushing her toward freedom and letting her forget the "crushing failures in my past" (100). In one splendid passage, Angelou, in an exultant style, again describes the dancing narrator: "The music was my friend, my lover, my family." In a series of comparisons she writes that dance music is a bright day, a happy son, poetry recited in a "warm bath" (112). What Maya needs for emotional sustenance she obtains by tapping her feet to the rhythm of the music.

Much of her style, though, reflects a negativity of moods and cadences. She describes the heights of a love affair, only to fall; she depicts the uncontrollable laughter that comes from smoking grass, only to crash. After she is fired for interfering in the boxing match, her language vividly records her depression. Guy's smile no longer moves her. She has lost her strength and her courage. Her marijuana is all gone. She feels "defenseless" for the very first time (175). The negativity of Angelou's style near the end of the book, immediately before she meets Troubadour Martin, suggests that Maya is looking for a way out, probably through drugs. Her style is slow, measured, in preparation for the trip to the lower depths that ends the volume.

The descent into the underworld has been a literary device in European literature since Homor's *The Odyssey*, when Odysseus, the epic hero, goes to the land of Hades and learns about the value of life from the slain Greek hero, Achilles: "Better, I say, to break sod as a farm hand . . . than lord it over all the exhausted dead" (Homer in *Norton Anthology of World Masterpieces* 1995, 344). Like Achilles and Odysseus, Troubadour Martin shows Maya a vision of hell that serves as an affirmation of life. By shooting up before her eyes, Troub proves to her that the drug high, which looks like paradise, is really the ultimate dead end. Realizing that "one man's generosity pushed me safely away from the edge," Maya regains her footing and vows to change the course of her life (181).

Troubadour's name has literary association as well. During the Middle Ages (1200–1400), troubadours were musician-poets from the south of France. Inspired by lyric poems from the Greeks, troubadours resided in royal courts or wandered the countryside, composing words and music. Given the idea of music as salvation in *Gather Together*, it seems that Troubadour Martin behaves like a soothing musician in keeping Maya away from the turmoil of drug addiction. Angelou admits that Troubadour Martin is not his real name, but that the episode was accurate: "[I]n the bathroom he made me stand there and watch as he tied himself up and then probed for a place which would accept . . . and he had scars so that . . . Oh God, it was so awful" ("Icon" 1997).

Other critics have noticed parallels between *Gather Together* and Greek literature, especially to the Persephone-Demeter myth of Greek mythology. Elizabeth Fox-Genovese (1990) remarks that *Gather Together in My Name* is a reimaging of the Persephone myth in which a daughter, Persephone, is raped and kidnapped by Hades, the god of the underworld. Her mother, Demeter, goddess of agriculture, grieves so deeply that all of nature becomes barren. To save the world from complete starvation, Hades permits his bride to visit Demeter for half of the year. For the other half Persephone must return to Hades. This profound attachment between mother and daughter, one of the very few woman-oriented myths in Greek legend, explains the power of mother love and accounts for the change of the seasons. Stephanie A. Demetrakopoulous (1980) develops the parallel more fully in her study of symbols of the mother in four American autobiographies.

Angelou may have the Demeter/Persephone myth in mind in her treatment of the mother/daughter theme in *I Know Why the Caged Bird Sings* and *Gather Together in My Name*. Maya's rape in *Caged Bird* initiates a five-year separation between mother and daughter and thrusts Maya into a hell of silence that is alleviated by another mother figure, Mrs. Flowers, whose name indicates springtime and fertility. Reunited at last with her mother, Vivian Baxter, Maya nonetheless leaves her at the beginning of the second volume. She descends into a world of prostitution, visits the underworld with Troubadour Martin as her guide, and finally emerges with the promise to return to her mother. While the Persephone story is to some degree relevant to Maya's situation, the mythological reading fails to take into account Vivian Baxter's remoteness in both volumes. Nor does it address Maya's primary emotional commitment, which is not to Vivian, the mother, but to her son.

A WOMANIST READING

Maya Angelou has been more than eloquent in writing about the conditions of black women in America. Near the end of *I Know Why the Caged Bird Sings*, she presents several moving paragraphs on the subject, from the point of view of a high-school student who has stopped attending classes but continues to learn and observe. Angelou argues that the black woman is entangled by her own nature as well as by three powerful enemies: "masculine prejudice, white illogical hate, and Black lack of power." The black woman who survives these opponents merits "respect if not enthusiastic acceptance" (231).

Angelou published these comments in 1970. Almost three decades later she wrote in a similar vein that the "heartbreaking tenderness of black women and their majestic strength" are responsible for black women's survival (*Stars* 44). Each of these passages speaks to the "womanist" issues raised in *Gather Together in My Name*: masculine bias, white racism, women's lack of power, and women's tenderness, strength, and survival.

"Womanist" is a more appropriate term than "feminist" for identifying Angelou's attitudes towards black women in *Gather Together*. Novelist Alice Walker popularized the term womanist in the introductory section of *In Search of Our Mothers' Gardens* (1967), to make explicit the

racial distinctions between black feminists and white feminists. A womanist is a "black feminist or feminist of color," wrote Walker. "Womanist
is to feminist as purple is to lavender." The color purple indicates
strength, power, and woman/love, what Walker calls "being grown up,"
as opposed to the less forceful, lavender qualities of the white feminist
movement. According to Deborah King, a "womanist is spirited and
spiritual, determined and decisive, committed to struggle and convinced
of victory" (qtd. in Tierney 1991, 390).

Black women in America committed themselves to the struggle for
civil rights well over one hundred years ago, in associations such as the
Afric-American Female Intelligence Society of Boston and the more
broadly based National Association of Colored Women. If black women
have not displayed a great interest in feminism as defined since the 1970s
by white women, it is because of racism in the women's movement,
claims Deborah King, who outlines the three major items on the womanist agenda: first, establishing positive images among black women;
second, recognizing that race, class, and gender play a part in the oppression of black women; and third, awareness of the cultural heritage
of black women (qtd. in Tierney 1991, 42–44).

With her focus on positive self-image, race, gender, and black women's
heritage, Maya Angelou fits the cultural definition of "womanist" far
more comfortably than she fits the category of "feminist." Although she
does not ascribe to labels, she did tell one interviewer that if she was a
female she was of course a feminist. "I'd be stupid not to be on my own
side" (Forma 1989, 162).

Because *Gather Together* takes place in the mid-1940s, Maya has no
contact with the theories of either womanism or feminism, neither of
which became significant to women's thinking until 1963, when Betty
Friedan published her explosive book, *The Feminine Mystique*, arguing
that women did not need to be tied exclusively to the roles of mother
and homemaker. In many ways, Angelou's life has been a constant struggle to prove, long before Betty Friedan, that she could have a career as
well as a child, although the immature eighteen-year-old protagonist of
Gather Together was hardly thinking in such sophisticated terms. A single
mother needed a job; it was that simple.

Maya's sense of being a black woman centers on economic survival.
In her effort to stay afloat, she epitomizes Walker's definition of a womanist as one who often exhibits "outrageous, audacious, courageous or
willful behavior" (1967, xi, emphasis Walker's). One example of Maya's
outrageous behavior is her slick-talking proposal to Johnnie Mae and

Beatrice that they set up a whorehouse with Maya as the Madam. With no prior experience, with no idea of the legal consequences, Maya acts outrageously and audaciously in manipulating the two women. At the same time, she is courageous when she interrupts L. D. Tolbrook at home, demanding that he help her retrieve her son, kidnapped by Big Mary Dalton.

According to Alice Walker's fourth quality of womanism, a womanist is *willful*, in this sense indicating a positive expression of the black self. As a womanist Maya shows strong evidence of being stubborn. From her initial decision to leave her mother to her final decision to return, Maya acts in a self-determined way. At times she fantasizes about being married and protected, but she rejects these dreams as unrealistic. For the most part, she directs her own course of events. She willfully disrupts a prizefight when a friend is beaten, knowing she will lose her job. She willfully challenges the salesgirl in Stamps who blocks her way, knowing she may lose her grandmother's affection. She willfully decides to give up all thoughts of heroin after she witnesses Troubadour's undoing, knowing that if she doesn't she may lose her life. In her willfulness, Maya at eighteen is a forerunner of Walker's womanist model: "Responsible. In charge. *Serious*" (1967, xi, Walker's emphasis).

5

Singin' and Swingin' and Gettin' Merry Like Christmas
(1976)

When Angelou's second volume, *Gather Together in My Name,* reached its conclusion, Maya, luckily released from a life of drug addiction and prostitution, vowed to maintain her innocence. In the following, volume *Singin' and Swingin' and Gettin' Merry Like Christmas,* Maya, now in her early twenties, displays a sense of self-rejection that negates the more positive ending of *Gather Together.* She's too tall, too skinny. Her teeth stick out. Her hair is "kinked" (4). She is distrustful of people who show an interest in her. How similar this portrait is to the beginning of *I Know Why the Caged Bird Sings,* where she believes herself to be ugly and deplores her ruffled purple dress. The description is also reminiscent of negative self-image in other autobiographies by African American women, for example in the early pages of Zora Neale Hurston's *Dust Tracks on a Road* (1942), or in the racial confusion experienced by bell hooks when her parents gave her white dolls when she longed for "unwanted, unloved brown dolls covered in dust" (1996, 24).

For the lonely Maya, the major escape is contemporary music. She frequently visits a record store on Fillmore Street in Los Angeles, a place with turntables and stalls for listening to the newest records. Here she is befriended by a white woman, Louise Cox, who offers the suspicious Maya a job. Here she meets her first husband, Tosh Angelos.

Throughout this troubled autobiography, Angelou's emotions are focused on her son, Guy. She marries Tosh Angelos, in part to please her son. But the marriage is not workable and ends in divorce. Maya is once again a single mother—once again the person responsible for Guy's needs, his well-being, his survival. Her achievements and failures as a mother-identified woman conflict with her aspirations for a career. These antagonisms form a pattern of tensions in this, Angelou's most complex volume.

Angelou's conflicts are concentrated in three basic areas: her marriage; her responsibilities as a mother, daughter, and granddaughter; and her desire to experience the joy of her self. Two incidents in particular contribute to the feelings of dissatisfaction that permeate the book. One is the death of Maya's beloved grandmother, Momma Henderson, the other is Angelou's characterization of herself as someone out of tune, someone whose confusion over priorities leads her to certain regrettable errors in judgment. In the final scene, set in Hawaii, these uncertainties are partially resolved.

NARRATIVE POINT OF VIEW

Singin' and Swingin' and Gettin' Merry Like Christmas marks an historical moment in the history of African American autobiography. At this time, no other well-known black female autobiographer had taken her story into a third volume. Maya Angelou's decision to keep going affects point of view, for there is now a narrator who is telling her life story in three distinct but connected segments, each linked to the other by the changing central character and by the first-person point of view. In extending her story into a third frame, Angelou deviates from the more contained autobiographical pattern, which tends to begin in a moment of revelation and to end at some decisive moment in the autobiographer's life, as in *Black Elk Speaks* (1932), which begins in boyhood and ends in the emptiness of reservation life following the 1890 massacre of the Sioux nation at Wounded Knee. Black Elk's story has a strong sense of tradition; the narrator relies on established cultural myths and dream figures, using repetition in order to affirm the importance of Native American life. *Singin' and Swingin'* lacks this kind of assured uniformity.

During an interview Angelou seemed very concerned that her serial autobiography did not result in repetition: "Somehow, if one thing tells the truth and were able to say it, then that thing is enough. You don't have to tell it again and again. If you've told it so delicious that it seeped in by osmosis, then you've done it" ("Icon" 1997). Osmosis is defined as a process in which a fluid passes through a cell wall or some other lining, leading to a spreading or diffusion of liquids. For Angelou to use that concept to explain the writing process, especially when she needs to structure multiple volumes of material, seems to indicate a lack of control. Later in the interview she did acknowledge the need to consciously repeat certain material: "Some things which are repetitive can be boring and really not serve you well. Some things, on the other hand, which seem to make the point again, if they are extended or if another color is put in, are okay because that does drive the point" ("Icon" 1997).

Angelou's third installment reveals her good traits while also exposing her weaker ones, so that what emerges is the familiar narrator who has become more dynamic, more open. Her use of flashbacks and flashforwards enables her to move up and down the narrative scale, for instance, when she recalls Momma Henderson selling meat pies to workers or Vivian Baxter making good money as she "ran businesses and men with autocratic power" (11). Both recollections extend the point of view from an individual to a collective one; it is not only Angelou's pride that is at stake, it is the family's. The Baxters and Johnsons exercised "unlimited authority" in their financial affairs (10), to the point that welfare is not a job alternative. The narrator's memories of her enterprising family members serve as connective threads, helping to create a sense of unity among the individual volumes of the series.

STRUCTURE AND SETTING

Throughout this work structure is defined as an arrangement of the story according to the motif of movement or travel, while setting is the number of locations where specific events unfold. The first two volumes occupy a varied American setting represented by Arkansas, Missouri, and California. In *Singin' and Swingin'* the setting breaks open, shifting from its American focus to include a European location. The expanded setting continues throughout the remaining autobiographies: volume 4, *The Heart of a Woman*, takes place in California, New York, Europe, and Egypt; volume 5, *All God's Children Need Traveling Shoes*, ends in West Africa and anticipates Angelou's return to America.

The movement from one journey to another establishes the narrative form, both in the single volume and in the series as a whole, with interconnected routes denoting places where action occurs. Thus, the scattered adventures into song, dance, and men that give *Gather Together in My Name* its chaotic structure are more organized and tightened up in *Singin' and Swingin'*, where the most sustained journey is Angelou's European adventure.

In 1954, Maya becomes the lead dancer with the touring company of *Porgy and Bess*. Her extensive coverage of the tour, which accounts for about 40 percent of the third volume, indicates how very important it was to her life. On the European tour, Angelou carefully details the course of travel, dividing the journey into subgroups: the plane to Milan; the bus from the Milan airport; the fast train or Blue Train from Venice to Paris; the astounded crowd preventing her movement in Yugoslavia; and so forth. In recording her momentous journey, Angelou's point of view is that of an aware and articulate black woman who does not hesitate to make racial generalizations. Angelou is quite conscious, for instance, of the white personnel in European hotels, and how they react to the lively African American cast. She listens to a wealthy white French woman, who remarks that West Africans living in Paris are hated but black Americans are not. She notices that Italians tend to approve of black Americans but not white ones (147). Her observations of race, gender, and class, along with the personality that she brings to every situation, prevent *Singin' and Swingin'* from becoming a travel narrative.

Angelou agrees that the theme of the journey becomes increasingly significant and somber in the last book, *Even the Stars Look Lonesome*. The author illustrates her theme not in its literary sense but through the tortured journey of her friend and burn victim Betty Shabazz, whose doctors could not understand her phenomenal fight against death. We need to learn from her struggle, Angelou commented, about the widow of Malcolm X: "But there's something about the journey, the onerous climb. It may be part of the lesson to learn. I imagine that each of us is on a journey" ("Icon" 1997).

So varied a set of journeys helps create the sense of flux or change in the series. Imagine that Maya had stayed in Stamps, Arkansas, for her entire life, had gotten a job as a school teacher, and had married the manager of the lumber mill. Although there might still be an autobiography as intense as *I Know Why the Caged Bird Sings*, it would have ended there and would not have become a series, a structure that is dependent on changes in setting, values, and culture.

PLOT DEVELOPMENT

The plot of *Singin' and Swingin'* is not a progressive action from beginning to end, like the plot of a standard novel, but rather a sequence
of conflicts or oppositions that emerge, recede, and often disappear from
the text, only to be revived pages later in a different form.

The construction of the plot of Angelou's third autobiography is best
described as the effective placement of opposing incidents and attitudes.
Singin' and Swingin' and Gettin' Merry Like Christmas explores a variety
of issues affecting Angelou's life—from motherhood, making a living,
being a wife, being a grandchild. In almost every instance Angelou's
attitude toward these and other issues is ambivalent, what some people
call the "Yes, But Syndrome" and others the "Affirmation/Denial Syndrome."

At the beginning of the volume, Angelou is in her twenties, struggling
to provide herself and her son with fundamental needs but unwilling to
go on welfare. She is offered a job selling records, which she wants to
do, but she distrusts the white woman who owns the store. She takes
the job. At the shop she meets a Greek sailor whose knowledge of black
music is equal to her own. She wants to marry him, but she is suspicious.
He is white but he is also Greek. She marries him but there are conflicts.
They divorce.

Angelou's great love is for her son Guy, but she also needs a chance
for her career to grow. She leaves Guy with her mother, Vivian Baxter,
and dances in Europe, Yugoslavia, and Egypt. But while she is overseas
she always misses her son. Vivian tells Maya that she has taken a job as
a dealer in Las Vegas and that there's no one to care for Guy. Maya
leaves the tour, giving one month's notice, although she wants to stay.
At the end she is reunited with her son, but he is sick. They go to Hawaii
together. The story is finished.

This skeletal summary of the plot demonstrates how the patterns of
affirmation and denial protrude from the flesh of the autobiography,
advancing the plot while at the same time retarding it. The pattern of
"yes, buts" or denials is the bare bones of the plot. Once the reader
recognizes what Angelou is doing, sometimes with awareness, sometimes not, he/she will gain a new appreciation for her dialectical
method—a critical term to indicate a construction or arrangement based
on a conflict of opposites. This dialectic is particularly relevant to the

characterization of black motherhood, introduced in the childhood narrative, but finding its fullest expression in *Singin' and Swingin' and Gettin' Merry Like Christmas*.

CHARACTER DEVELOPMENT

The term "conflict of opposites" appropriately describes the character development in *Singin' and Swingin' and Gettin' Merry Like Christmas*. Character development in a standard, single-volume autobiography, for example in Richard Wright's *Black Boy* (1945), reflects a clear and consistent pattern of behavior that shows growth and change in the narrator from the beginning until the conclusion. In Angelou's extended series, though, the central character, rather than being a self-directed autobiographer, frequently demonstrates qualities of self-negation/self-acceptance as she vacillates back and forth between denying and accepting her self. This wavering of character from one volume to another is most extreme in *Singin' and Swingin' and Gettin' Merry Like Christmas*, where Maya's personality is often ambiguous: uncertain, indefinite, and unsettled. And yet, it is because of these negative characteristics that Angelou engages readers in the awesome reality of her personality. She is a woman who dramatically demonstrates that the self-conscious narrator can be aware of her mistakes.

In the construction of an autobiography, character and plot are almost inseparable. The character of the narrator is married to the plot as decisions are made or postponed, unions are done or undone, children are sent away or kept at one's side. Both Angelou and the other characters in *Singin' and Swingin'* often surmount the oppositional forces that divide them. Indeed, there are moments of exhilaration. But even her great success in *Singin' and Swingin'*, the *Porgy and Bess* tour, for example, has its down side.

The elation implied in the title is contradicted by other, discordant experiences that play for and against each other in the formation of Angelou's character. Confused, uncentered, she is forced to make a number of choices concerning her mothering, her profession, and her sexuality. Her character develops as she confronts these choices, which involve the people she is closest to: her son, her grandmother, her mother, her brother, her husband, her self.

The first significant circumstance affecting her character is her relationship with Tosh Angelos. Maya meets her husband-to-be early in the third autobiography, when she is a salesgirl in a record store. Impressed by the young sailor's enthusiasm for jazz, she introduces him to Guy, who is immediately won over. Vivian Baxter is not. She warns Maya against marrying Tosh because he is a "poor white man" (24). Maya, though, evades that problem by telling herself Tosh is really Greek, not white.

The marriage is initially satisfying, but eventually Maya begins to resent Tosh's demands that she stay at home and be the perfect housewife, the provider of suitable meals and "fabulous jello desserts" (26). She is also bothered by what she senses as disapproval from her friends because of the interracial marriage. As Tosh takes greater control of her life, Maya, who "mistakes prison for security," does little to challenge his authority (McPherson 1990, 83).

The conflict between Maya and Tosh centers on two issues: gender roles and religion. When Tosh tells Guy that there is no God, Maya is furious. She reacts by secretly visiting black churches, searching for the faith she left behind in Stamps with Momma Henderson. She is also looking for a way to get back at Tosh. Her quest ends in her conversion at the Evening Star Baptist Church, in one of the first great celebrations of African American culture in the series. The shouts, gospels, spirituals, "polyrhythmic" clapping of hands all converge on Angelou "like sweet oil" as she shakes with elation (28).

The religious transformation, like the marriage, is short-lived. The differences between Maya and Tosh grow until one day he says he's "tired of being married" (37). In a quiet rage that last for several pages, Maya ponders the issue of race, fantasizing that Tosh is a member of the Ku Klux Klan. Using her sexuality as revenge, she goes to a bar, gets smashed, and spends the night with an older man, knowing that Guy will be safe with his stepfather. When she returns home her attitude towards Tosh has changed. She is no longer the perfect housewife, cook, or cooperative lover. Maya loses her affection for him, and the marriage of nearly three years collapses.

The second struggle that strongly influences her character is the conflict within the family: between Maya and her son Guy; between Maya and her mother; between Maya and her paternal grandmother. The mother/son conflict is intensified by Maya's guilt over not being a responsible mother. Social standards determine that a good mother is faithful and ever-caring. Social standards dictate that a good mother is one who sacrifices her own happiness for that of her child, who makes no move that disrupts her child's friendships or schooling.

The complicated issue of motherhood is a unifying but also a disruptive theme throughout the series and one that receives its own treatment in the Thematic Issues section of this chapter. In terms of character development, the mother/child opposition is an essential aspect of Angelou's growth. She said in an interview that "the absolutely greatest thing that happened to me was my son, because I had to grow and learn not to smother him" (Toppman 1989, 144). She seems to be searching for the right balance: neither smothering nor slighting him.

Because of her year's absence from Guy, Maya suffers during the primary action of the volume, the company tour of *Porgy and Bess*. When the tour is over, Maya makes a vow to her son never to leave him again. On that promise the book ends.

Maya's relationship with her mother, Vivian Baxter, takes on new dimensions in *Singin' and Swingin'*. Recall that at the end of *Gather Together in My Name*, Maya had returned to Vivian and Daddy Clidell for comfort, love, and lodging. When the subsequent volume, *Singin' and Swingin'*, opens, Maya is living an impoverished but independent life. She and Guy again return to the protection of her mother and stepfather's house on the condition that Maya pays a fair share of the expenses. Although happy with this arrangement, she is forced to retract it when, against Vivian's advice, she marries Tosh.

A few years later, after their divorce and the invitation to perform in *Porgy and Bess*, Maya relies on Vivian to take care of Guy while she is on tour. At this point Maya becomes aware of the comparison between Vivian, who left her children with their grandmother in Stamps, and Maya, who left her child with his grandmother in San Francisco. She is in effect echoing her own unhealthy child/mother experience, not because she wants to but because, despite the pain, she has to work. In a promise to herself that does not quite ring true, she claims: "I would make it up to my son and one day would take him to all the places I was going to see" (129).

In a further imitation of her mother, the absent Maya sends money to Vivian from Paris, asking her to buy Guy a present but to tell him his mother had sent it: "Then perhaps he would forgive my absence" (157). Maya thus copies her mother's actions when in *I Know Why the Caged Bird Sings* Vivian sends her daughter the hateful blonde doll that she subsequently destroys. While she is very much indebted to her mother for being willing to care for Guy while she is in Europe, the downside of such well-meaning child care is that Maya starts feeling guilty. She confesses that she sends home most of her pay to support her son and to "assuage my guilt at being away from him" (153).

A third confrontation, this one with her grandmother, Annie Henderson, is discreetly presented. The conflict occurs outside of the narrative, after Tosh informs Maya of Annie's death, to which she reacts in a dazzling passage three paragraphs long. Momma, the foremost influence in Maya's development, vanishes from her autobiographies—no longer able to comfort Maya or introduce Guy to the church; no longer able to caution her about racism. Momma Henderson's death is a major source for the feelings of futility in *Singin' and Swingin'*. The death of Maya's grandmother underscores a problem that Angelou never seems fully to come to terms with in the autobiographical series: her ambivalent feelings toward those she loves, including her mother; her father; her husband Tosh; and, in *Singin' and Swingin'*, Momma Henderson.

In writing about her grandmother's death, Angelou shifts from her generally more conversational tone and becomes passionate, religious, emotional: "Ah, Momma," she cries, lamenting that even if she were as "pure" as the Virgin Mary, she would never feel Momma Henderson's hands touch her face again (41). This moving farewell is not typical of Angelou's writing. Her words here betray a conflict, as if she is trying too hard, as if her guilt at having forgotten Momma is causing excessive emotions. The three-paragraph passage is a funeral elegy, a prose poem, a gem cemented within the narrative. As a poem, it relies on gospel tradition, on the language of Bible stories, and on certain African American literary texts, especially James Weldon Johnson's "Go Down Death—A Funeral Sermon" (1966).

Angelou's farewell to her black grandmother in this passage contains other refrains from the past. She longs to have Momma's "rough slow hands pat my cheek" (41). In terms of conflict, these hands are the ones that slapped Maya on the face for having sassed two white saleswomen in *Gather Together*. That slap, the bad slap that ended Maya's relationship with Momma, is changed in the funeral elegy to a good slap, a soft tap on the cheek. The two different slaps are a perfect example of what has been described as the conflict of opposites, frequently stated in *Singin' and Swingin' and Gettin' Merry Like Christmas*—the good/bad mother. Angelou's lament throughout these paragraphs also softens, as she expresses the wish to be "as good as God's angels" and as "pure as the Mother of Christ." Both metaphors are aspects of the good/bad conflict, in which Angelou attempts to deal with her guilt toward her grandmother and seek a loving reconciliation, if not here, then in the Hereafter.

In *Singin' and Swingin'* Angelou is extremely quiet not only about her grandmother's death but also about the fate of her brother, Bailey Johnson. In both cases she hides a major autobiographical relationship in a private, unreachable place. As if to emphasize her distance from Bailey, Maya mentions the letters he sends her from prison while she is in Europe, which Maya shares with her mother on her return to America. Maya remarks coldly that his touching stories about life in prison "left me unmoved" (233). That she is "unmoved" is at least one solution to the problem of the conflict of opposites, for if one feels nothing there is no conflict. One imagines that Angelou, after her shocking collision with drugs and drug addicts at the end of *Gather Together*, would like to put those experiences behind her. But Angelou says that the minimal information regarding Bailey is protective. She is doing what he asked: "Don't use my name in books." She added, "I am also silent for his protection" ("Icon" 1997).

Bailey is again mentioned near the end of *Singin' and Swingin'*, where Angelou tells us he is in Sing Sing prison for "fencing stolen goods" (234). His name appears for the last time in the series in *The Heart of a Woman*. She does not talk to him directly but mentions to Martin Luther King Jr. that her brother is in jail. Dr. King advises her to keep on loving her brother, reminding her that Bailey has more freedom of spirit than those who imprisoned him.

One final area of conflict for Angelou—and in many ways the primary one—is her interior struggle as she attempts to identify her life and desires and defend them against other, albeit important demands from the outside. It has been a hard struggle getting recognition as a dancer, something she has been trying to do since she was part of the dancing team of Poole and Rita, described in *Gather Together*. Aware that she has talent, Maya has been unlucky at finding a job in the entertainment business that will offer decent pay and some respectability. She had been dancing in bars and stripjoints as artistic backup for the more exotic showgirls. She had put in time as a B-girl—a woman who entices men to buy her watered-down bar drinks or cheap champagne at high prices. As in *Gather Together*, these scenes of the low life provide glimpses of a seedy underworld as Angelou wears sequined G-strings and the text approaches pornography, so stimulating is Angelou's language and descriptive power.

Maya is performing an assortment of dances and ballads in local cafes, including the calypso, a popular kind of rhythmic music that originated in Trinidad in the West Indies. Her big break comes when, at the intervention of some friends, she is invited to perform calypso music at the Purple Onion, a cabaret in the North Beach section of San Francisco, where at one point she shares the show with comedian Phyllis Diller.

Following the successful stint at the Purple Onion, she receives other offers, including the tempting proposal to replace Eartha Kitt in the 1954 musical, *New Faces*. She accepts instead the primary dancing role in *Porgy and Bess* for its European engagement of 1954–1955. This is a true victory, the foundation for her later performances in dance, theater, and song.

The strain of the *Porgy and Bess* tour takes away from Maya emotionally almost as much as it gives her professionally. Dolly A. McPherson writes that *Porgy and Bess* is like an "antagonist that enthralls Angelou, beckoning and seducing her away from her responsibilities" (1990, 85). McPherson's use of the word "antagonist" captures the oppositional aspect of the European tour and its pull on Angelou's loyalties. Sometimes an antagonist is not a person but instead an internal conflict that exists within an individual. This distinction is applicable to Angelou's internal, at-war personality.

The European travel-sequence has a great effect on both plot and character as Maya's absence generates a tug-of-war between Guy at home and his mother in Europe. Travel is a magnet that contributes to the overall tension of the narrative, a tension that momentarily ends with Maya's return to her son. When she arrives home after an exhausting boat and train trip, she learns that Guy is suffering from a skin disease that appears to have emotional causes. Promising never to leave him again, she takes him with her to Hawaii, where she has a singing engagement. In the last pages of *Singin' and Swingin'*, Angelou vows to Guy that she will never leave him, using words that are both simple and oppositional: "If I go, you'll go with me or I won't go" (232).

This volume closes in a sentence that highlights, through three nouns, the opposing tensions Angelou's temperament: "Although I was not a great singer I was his mother, and he was my wonderful, dependently independent son" (242). Again, the dialectical construct is apparent: I/ you; singer/mother; dependent/independent; mother/son. This sentence effectively concludes the first three books in its thumbnail summary of the major contradictions in Angelou's character. At the same time, it alludes to similar mother/son patterns in future volumes.

Angelou's writing in the third volume is brilliant, its strength deriving in part from the way in which she duplicates the actual conflicts underlying the plot, characters, and thought patterns. This kind of development is also found in *Hunger of Memory* (1982), an autobiography by Mexican American writer Richard Rodriguez, who examines the opposition between his Catholic-Mexican family and his alienated, Anglo-centered education. Maxine Hong Kingston's *Woman Warrior* (1976), also

looks deeply into class and familial conflicts in the clash between her
Chinese and American upbringing. Not many other contemporary autobiographers have been able to capture, either in a single volume or in
a series, the opposition of desires that is found in *Singin' and Swingin'
and Gettin' Merry Like Christmas* and, to a lesser extent, in Angelou's other
volumes.

THEMATIC ISSUES

The theme of maturing motherhood evolves in the second volume,
Gather Together, and continues in *Singin' and Swingin'*. The thematic issues of both volumes remain similar as Maya faces comparable problems
of parenting, relationships, and survival. All are pertinent to her role as
a single black mother determined to make a life for herself and her son
against a stacked deck—the obstacles of race and gender that for women
in the 1950s were in some cases insurmountable.

The major source of Angelou's anxiety in *Singin' and Swingin'* is her
temporary separation from her son, Guy. Much of Maya's struggle in
this, the most tangled of the autobiographies, concerns her private role
as a single mother versus her public role as a committed actress, one
whose career makes it necessary to leave Guy for long stretches of time.

Chosen to perform in the European tour of *Porgy and Bess*, she faces
the realization that in leaving Guy with his grandmother, she will repeat
the hateful pattern established by her parents when they left her and
Bailey in the hands of Momma Henderson. Her feelings are compounded
by the fact that, as a young, black, single mother, she bears the ultimate
responsibility for her son, whom she wants and needs to support. By
identifying the most fundamental conflict between working and mothering, Angelou presents a rare kind of literary model, the working
mother. This kind of model is becoming more and more essential as
women insist on both roles.

The mother/son behavior pattern in *Singin' and Swingin'* shows Guy
as the son seeking affection and Maya as the mother in conflict over the
need to love versus the need to be a fully realized person. This conflict,
as we saw earlier in the chapter, causes stress and indecision. One expects Maya, lead dance performer of the *Porgy and Bess* tour of Europe
and North Africa, to enjoy what her labor has earned. Instead, on almost
every page of description about Milan, Paris, or Venice, there appears a
lament about Guy that shuts off her positive experiences. On seeing

French children playing outside the train window, she writes: "The long-ing for my own son threatened to engulf me" (191). When she comes home to discover Guy's skin scaling from disease she says, "I had ruined my beautiful son by neglect, and neither of us would ever forgive me" (233).

It is not until she takes Guy to Hawaii that mother and son get a clearer perspective. She is his mother and she is a celebrity. He is her son and he needs her nurturing. Although Angelou avoids a fairytale-perfect ending, she gives readers, at this middle stage of her autobio-graphical series, a glimmer of the Maya Angelou to come and a tangible sense of the personal price she has paid for the opportunity. Although at the end of *Singin' and Swingin'* her exploration of the rewards and pains of motherhood appears to have been temporarily resolved, An-gelou continues to unfold the tensions between career and motherhood in the remaining two volumes.

Directly and indirectly related to the motherhood issue is the theme of music. "Music" is the the first word to follow the epigraph: "Music was my refuge" (1). As the word music opens the narrative, the idea of song (singin') and dance (swingin') dominates the title. Then, as if to leave no doubt in the reader's mind about the importance of music, An-gelou introduces the volume with an epigraph, as she introduced *I Know Why the Caged Bird Sings* with the line: "What you looking at me for?"

An epigraph is a short poem or prose piece, which sets the tone of the work that follows, usually by making a connection to the theme. In *Sin-gin' and Swingin'*, the epigraph is a quotation from an unidentified three-line stanza in classic blues form. For the first two lines, the blues singer asks if the moon is lonesome. The third line asks: "Don't your house look lonesome when your baby / pack up to leave?" In conventional blues, the word baby means lover. In this case however, Angelou changes the usual meaning to refer to her leaving Guy for a job in Eu-rope, and to leaving her mother for an independent life. The poignant words and rhythms are related to at least three of the major themes of the autobiography—motherhood, separation, and music. In terms of genre, it is important to note that by way of the epigraph, music, not poetry or fiction, introduces the reader to the narrative.

The lonely Maya, who initially finds solace in the cool notes of black music, later in the same volume discovers that music, highlighted in the title as singin' and swingin, offers her economic opportunity and the chance to be married. Her first daytime job is in a music store. She meets Tosh Angelos while selling records, falling for him when she discovers that his love for Charlie Parker, Dexter Gordon, and other jazz musicians is genuine. Later Maya excels in her singing and dancing performances, winning engagements in quality clubs because of her accomplishments in music.

The structure of *Singin' and Swingin'* is related to musical composition. By looking at the doubling of plot lines (Maya the mother/Maya the B-girl) as being associated with Angelou's use of opposition—pitting one force (good mother) against another, contrasting force (bad mother)—it is possible to see that Angelou uses certain kinds of music, especially jazz, that are based on similar oppositions. Such music is "polyphonic," where more than one line works in opposition to another. In *Singin' and Swingin'* certain perplexing issues touch each other and disconnect, so that the overall effect resembles a jazz composition. Angelou's narrative is constantly playing certain discordant or polyphonic notes. Thus, Vivian Baxter's dominant tones are pitted against her daughter's more tentative ones, or Tosh's loud cursing contends against Maya's silent rage.

The use of music is also effective in the funeral sermon for Momma Henderson. Angelou's sad notes are heard as she struggles to record the death of her now silent grandmother. To produce the desired effect, she uses the tones of the Negro spiritual to reach into eternity for her grandmother. At the end of the sermon Angelou cries that death is real "only in song" (42). Although such attention to music is observable in each of the volumes, it is only in *Singin' and Swingin'* and *Gather Together* that the musical theme affects the development of plot, structure, and character.

STYLE AND LITERARY DEVICES

Angelou achieves her powerful effects in *Singin' and Swingin' and Gettin' Merry Like Christmas* through a number of literary devices. First is her use of repetition. Angelou uses the current time period, the 1950s, to reflect on earlier events, repeating certain details in order to enhance the style. The most dramatic use of repetition is Angelou's leaving her son with Vivian Baxter, repeating the incident from her childhood when Vivian left Maya and Bailey with Momma Henderson. Another example is Maya's turning to the older man in the bar for sympathy during a crisis, as she turned to her older lover, Troubadour Martin, in *Gather Together*. From a psychological perspective, she may be repeating her need for Bailey Johnson, the father who once abandoned her. Her technique is reinforced through repeating certain words such as "confront" (43); "the past" (129); and "absence" (156).

Another stylistic technique that Angelou puts to excellent use is the simile, a comparison between two objects that is directly expressed through the presence of the words "like" or "as." Although there are a number of similes in *Singin' and Swingin'*, several deserve special attention. First is the explosion of images surrounding her religious conversion. In a further reference to the theme of music, she describes the Negro spirituals as "sweeter than sugar." Angelou further expands this straightforward simile into an elaborate image of her connections to the oral tradition of black culture. In other words, much of African American tradition derives from slave narratives and gospels (see Chapter 2). In this image, Angelou's connection to her oral heritage is through her mouth—what she speaks, what she sings, and what she tastes. She praises the spirituals she heard during her conversion: "I wanted to keep my mouth full of them" (28). This image of fullness contrasts with Vivian Baxter's empty mouth in *Caged Bird*—Maya's fantasy of a dead Vivian, her face a vast empty O, and Maya's tears "like warm milk" (43) in the absence of a milk-giving mother.

When Angelou returns to San Francisco near the end of the autobiography she also expresses her confusion through the use of simile: "Disorientation hung in my mind like a dense fog" (232). The fog is contrasted with occasional moments of clarity: "clear as the clink of good crystal" (233), contrasting elements expressed in the images of clear crystal and fog. Through these two comparisons Angelou is exposing a confusion strong enough to make her hastily consult and then reject a prosperous-looking white psychiatrist.

Finally, Angelou likes to use the simile to humorous effect, especially when she is exaggerating certain clichés concerning black culture. For example, the cast of *Porgy and Bess* runs into Lionel Hampton's band at a reception in Israel (Hampton [b. 1913] is the first jazz artist to perform successfully on the vibraphone [Southern 1971, 495].) Angelou writes that the cast jumped on Hampton's band members "as if they were bowls of black-eyed peas" (216). This simile reveals the racial hunger that African Americans experienced during their white engagements. The hunger motif connects the black-eyed peas simile to black-skinned people and to the mouth full of sugar used to describe the spirituals. Each takes its meaning from an oral reference. The title of the third volume is also based on a simile: *Singin' and Swingin' and Gettin' Merry* LIKE *Christmas*.

A DECONSTRUCTIVE READING

In *Singin' and Swingin'*, Angelou, through her care for language and style, imaginatively renders the black experience from the perspective of a mother who is also a daughter. This chapter discusses the conflicting aspects of Maya's character—her tendency to represent herself in terms of indecisiveness or uncertainty. Emphasis on these conflicts is a modest form of deconstructive criticism. Deconstruction is a field of criticism heavily grounded in the linguistic theories of French philosophers Fernand de Saussure and Jacques Derrida, and is currently practiced by American critics such as Barbara Johnson and J. Hillis Miller.

One of the main assumptions of deconstruction is that language in itself has no fixed meaning, that a word or words have significance only as they are different from other words surrounding them. Therefore, it is necessary to give a work of literature—a novel, a poem, an autobiography—what is called a "close reading," the kind of probing verbal analysis that until the 1960s had been generally reserved for poetry. A close reading invariably leads the deconstructionist to the conclusion that the author has no claim to what the piece of writing means, that the text has no authority, and that there can be many, many meanings to words, none of them right and none of them wrong.

A critic committed to deconstruction scrutinizes the language of *Singin' and Swingin' and Gettin' Merry Like Christmas*, looking for evidence of uncertainty, of multiple meanings. Words, passages, and episodes are interpreted in a multitude of ways because the words of the text lean toward ambiguity and are therefore open to a deconstructive reading. The most radical application of the theory is that the deconstruction of the text has already happened before the critic approaches the material. The critic realizes that the "construct, by its very nature, has already undone, dismantled, or deconstructed itself" (Harmon and Holman 1996, 142).

A deconstructive reading of *Singin' and Swingin' and Gettin' Merry Like Christmas* might consider the implications of the title, which in its complexity of language reflects a multitude of meanings related to the text. First of all, to use an old-fashioned term, the title is ironic, meaning that the "actual intent is expressed in words that carry the opposite meaning" (Harmon and Holman 1996, 277). The title is composed of what might be assumed are positive words: "singin'," "swingin'," "Merry," "Christmas." But on closer inspection, singing and swinging are words that depict Angelou's career, words that at times signify success but at other times create such a vast distance and separation between herself and her son that when she returned home from Europe she contemplated "killing herself and possibly even the child" (234).

Although "Merry" and "Christmas" initially reflect happiness, these words, too, must be seen ironically as expressing the opposite meaning. *Singin' and Swingin' and Gettin' Merry Like Christmas* is Angelou's most unmerry autobiography. The reader who tries to understand the series as a whole may recall another Christmas and the bitter scene from *Caged Bird* in which the absent mother, Vivian Baxter, sends her black child a tea set and a blonde-haired white doll (just as the absent Maya sends Vivian money from Paris to purchase Guy a present in *Singin' and Swingin'*). Angelou writes that the next day she and her brother ripped the doll to shreds. These gifts appear to be metaphors for Maya's divided self, symbolized by the torn and unwanted doll. As she negates the doll, she negates her self.

In a telling passage from *The Heart of a Woman*, she uses a comparably negative scene in identifying the joys of Christmas when, at her first meeting of the Harlem Writers Guild, she is devastated by a group critique of her play. The judges attacked her and damaged her ego, but "now they were as cheery as Christmas cards" (40). Another pun on the word "Christmas" appears in *Gather Together in My Name*. Maya is talking to a prostitute who's "off the streets" because she was too hot. The woman says she's cooling down. "Then I'll be back switching and bitching and getting merry like Christmas" (137). The parallel between the whore's bragging in *Gather Together* (1974) and Angelou's title in *Singin' and Swingin'*, published four years later, is unmistakable.

There are several other associations between the title *Singin' and Swingin' and Gettin' Merry Like Christmas*, and the series. The word "merry" is a homonym, a word that is identical in pronunciation to another word but that has a different origin and meaning. "Merry" has the same sound as "Mary," a name with rich associations. In *Caged Bird* Maya is horribly offended when the white woman she works for, Mrs. Cullinan, keeps calling her "Mary" and not by her right name. One will also recall the significance of Big Mary Dalton in *Gather Together*. She is the baby-sitter who separates Maya from her son by kidnapping him. In *Singin' and Swingin'* the Mary figure is the Mother of Christ, the pure virgin of Maya's dreams. For each of these three Mary's there are surrounding implications of ambivalence and denial.

Two final suggestions come to mind in a deconstructive reading. First, Angelou intentionally changes the *ing* endings that indicate the present participle in standard English. In transforming the standard spellings into the slangy "singin'," "swingin'," and "gettin'," she jazzes up the

verbs like Henry Louis Gates Jr. does throughout his study of the "sig-
nifyin(g) monkey" (1988). Both writers create the sense of the black ver-
nacular, the sound of a down home blues singer by dropping the formal
"g." Second is Angelou's concern that her brother Bailey is in prison,
namely, Sing Sing. The *ing* sounds call Sing Sing to mind, if only in the
ironic name of the prison: Sing Sing is an unmerry place to be.

Angelou has an understandably different interpretation of the title. She
told an interviewer that the title *Singin' and Swingin' and Gettin' Merry
Like Christmas* derived from rent parties, Saturday night survival parties
popular in Harlem in the 1920s and 1930s. People payed their host a
quarter, then ate, drank, and were merry for the weekend. They would
"sing and swing and get merry like Christmas" (Angelou qtd. in Saunders 1991, 6).

Rent parties, also called "parlor socials," were swinging and merry,
full of fun and dance. Looking at the economic implications of rent parties, they were mainly attended by "laundry workers, seamstresses, por-
ters, elevator operators," and other members of the working class who
could not afford or could not have been admitted to the "classier Harlem
night spots" (Anderson 1981, 152–53). An indication of desperate economic conditions, rent parties were a communal solution for people who
could not afford to go to Harlem's expensive clubs. However, rent parties
did offer black musicians a place to be heard and were, according to
Jervis Anderson (1981), not native to Harlem but the continuation of a
Southern tradition. The concept of the rent party helps describe Angelou's position in volumes 2 and 3: she is a single mother from the South
who goes to California and sings and swings for a living. She entertains
others for little money as a singer, B-girl, and dancer, without getting
very merry at all.

That comes years later when Angelou finds her true voice through the
autobiographical narrative form. Her singing and swinging performances at the Purple Onion and her outstanding dancing in *Porgy and Bess*
bring her a good measure of the public recognition that will be her due
from now on, as indicated by her concert performances with the singers
Ashford and Simpson in the late 1990s. Her primary cultural role in
Singin' and Swingin' and Gettin' Merry Like Christmas is as a stage performer, not as a writer. As a person who dramatizes the songs and
dances of the African, Caribbean, and African American oral tradition,
she is giving dramatic expression to other people's words and music.
Not until volume 4, *The Heart of a Woman*, does she begin the difficult
task of giving voice to her own narrative.

6

The Heart of a Woman
(1981)

Like *Gather Together in My Name*, *The Heart of a Woman* opens with several paragraphs of historical reflection intended to locate the autobiographer in time and place. The book covers Maya's life from 1957 to 1962. At the beginning blacks and whites are enveloped in contradictions. The highly regarded tennis player, Althea Gibson, has become America's first black women's singles champion. In the same America, President Eisenhower dispatches federal troops to Arkansas, where black children and their parents are hoping to integrate the Little Rock school system.

In the more personal opening sequence of *The Heart of a Woman*, Angelou and her son Guy are living communally on a houseboat near San Francisco, trying to bridge the gap between black and white and living on the savings she has put away while singing in California and in Hawaii. Within a year, she and Guy move from the commune to a rented house near San Francisco and, finally, in 1959, they cross the continent to New York City.

In New York, Angelou, no longer satisfied with singing in nightclubs, dedicates herself to acting, writing, political organizing, and her son. She becomes involved with Martin Luther King's growing civil-rights organization, the Southern Christian Leadership Conference (SCLC), doing a significant fund-raiser for King and becoming a key organizer in his group. These activities make *The Heart of a Woman* the "most political segment of Angelou's autobiographical statement" (Cudjoe 1990, 297).

Her activities with SCLC cease shortly after Angelou meets Vusumzi Make, a handsome South African. After a wedding ceremony in London that is never legalized, Maya, Vus, and Guy move to Egypt. While living in Cairo, Maya discovers that Vus has been buying expensive items of furniture without her knowledge and that he has been unfaithful. After a public display of emotion, Maya leaves with Guy for West Africa, hoping that she might set up residence in Liberia. But en route, in Ghana, Guy is seriously injured in a car accident. On this event, which happened in 1962, *The Heart of a Woman* ends and the fifth volume, *All God's Children Need Traveling Shoes*, begins.

NARRATIVE POINT OF VIEW

The Heart of a Woman is the fourth volume in Angelou's continuing autobiography. Like the other volumes, it is narrated from the point of view of a mother/woman who tells much the same intimate story that she told in *Gather Together in My Name* and *Singin' and Swingin' and Gettin' Merry Like Christmas*—but with an enormous difference. By the time she is ready to present the fourth segment of her life story, Angelou has accumulated a multilayered memory that affects not only what she remembers but what readers who have followed her previous books remember. As a serial autobiographer she must continuously look backward unveiling the various layers hidden in earlier volumes, remembering what she has already written without being repetitious. Autobiographer Lillian Hellman named this process "pentimento," a term used in painting to indicate the reappearance of a design that has been covered over by layers of paint.

Of the many instances in which Angelou uses this layered point of view in *The Heart of a Woman*, perhaps the most effective is the incident in which she confronts Jerry, the leader of the Savages, a Brooklyn street gang that has threatened Guy because he reportedly hit Jerry's girlfriend. Enraged, a borrowed pistol in her purse, Angelou tells Jerry that if anything happens to Guy she will shoot him and his family, kill the grandmother, kill the baby, kill anything that "moves, including the rats and cockroaches" (84). Read from a multileveled point of view, Maya's violent reaction in this episode goes back to *Caged Bird*, back to her rape, and back to the vengeful actions that Grandmother Baxter and her family took against Mr. Freeman. Her violent behavior in handling Jerry may involve an unconscious effort to rewrite her own history. She will be aggressive, like the Baxters. She will not be passive, like her paternal grandmother, Momma Henderson, who hid Uncle Willie in the potato bin when the Ku Klux Klan arrived; who hummed submissively when the three offensive white girls taunted her in front of the store; who slapped Maya and sent her away in *Gather Together* because Maya challenged a white saleswoman. Maya will do whatever it takes to protect her son. At the same time, her aggression is played out against her fear that she cannot save Guy from harm, an attitude that reveals "the vulnerability she feels as a mother trying to protect her child from any form of danger" (Neubauer 1987, 128).

In addition to the multilayered point of view, another difference in point of view is determined by the narrator's changed self. *The Heart of a Woman* depends far less on the strategies of fiction than *Caged Bird* did; there is less use of dialogue and less reliance on dramatic episodes to convey action or emotion. Angelou unfolds the events affecting her in a more confident, less troubled manner. The young mother is now older and wiser, more capable of dealing with matters still confronting her. Although she remains to some degree distressed by the challenges of parenting, personal development, and survival, she nonetheless demonstrates significant personal growth in these areas. Part of her development comes from her political commitment. Her growing self-assurance, strengthened by her friendships within the Harlem Writers Guild and relationships with Godfrey Cambridge, Martin Luther King Jr., and other public figures, leads to her participation in African American and African protest rallies. Angelou attends a huge march in New York following the death of Prime Minister Lumumba, of Zaire. She also does fund-raising and organizational projects for Dr. King.

Although the narrator repeats and improvises on earlier motifs, *The Heart of a Woman* is considerably more uplifting than its predecessors, *Gather Together in My Name* and *Singin' and Swingin' and Gettin' Merry Like Christmas*. *Singin' and Swingin'* ended with Angelou questioning her authenticity and her status as a woman who let her singing career interfere with her duties as a mother. Her apparent resolution of the mother/child conflict was to subordinate the maternal self to the needful child.

In *The Heart of a Woman* there is a significant new direction in Angelou's story. She has gone from childbirth at the end of *Caged Bird*, to fragmented chaos and pain in being a mother in *Gather Together* and *Singin' and Swingin'*, to a book that for the first time affirms the achievement of a personal and public maturity. Additionally, in *The Heart of a*

Woman, Angelou enlarges the scope of autobiography in both form and content, providing it with a fourth dimension. By adding a fourth book to the series, she has conceived a multivolume narrative structure unsurpassed in American autobiography.

In presenting herself as a mature individual, Angelou approximates the perspective of classic American autobiography as described in *I Know Why the Caged Bird Sings*, in which works by Benjamin Franklin, Henry Adams, and others are said to provide models for successful living. In the fourth volume, Angelou, no longer a threatened Southern child, no longer a deluded prostitute or a fledgling dancer, is now in the position to offer direction to black women and men younger than herself, to be a model like many autobiographers before her. Where she differs from most male narrators, though, is that she is a "woman" with a woman's "heart." As such, Angelou is able to offer a woman's perspective as she reveals her concerns about her self-image and her conflicting feelings about her lovers and her son.

In the fourth segment of the five-part life story, *The Heart of a Woman* fulfills the mother/son narrative. Rich in theme and characterization, it represents the point of view of a prominent African American woman whose talents are in the service of humanity. She is engaged in the civil-rights movement, in political protest, in feminism, yet Angelou is also at her most introspective. *The Heart of a Woman* is an open, revelatory book; Angelou's feelings dictate the form. According to Dolly A. McPherson, *The Heart of a Woman* is an intensely truthful volume: "Her writing here, describing her longings, doubts, and shortcomings, is raw, bare honesty" (1990, 98).

STRUCTURE

Like all Angelou's narratives, the structure of *The Heart of a Woman* is based on a journey, from place to place, from house to house, from coast to coast. To emphasize the theme of movement, she opens the text by quoting from a spiritual that repeats the same line: "The ole ark's a-moverin'." The repeated reference to Noah's ark, an allusion to the Biblical narrative and Angelou's secret pursuit of Christianity in *Singin' and Swingin' and Gettin' Merry Like Christmas*, also heralds the motif of the journey. By implication, Maya Angelou is a new Noah, "a moverin' along" in the quest to survive, much as Janie Crawford, the powerful central woman character of Zora Neale Hurston's *Their Eyes Were Watch-*

ing God (1937), is a reincarnation of Noah in her survival of the flooding of Lake Okechobee.

On the first page of *The Heart of a Woman* Angelou makes a number of references to moving, as in her mention of Jack Kerouac's 1951 novel *On the Road*. Kerouac (1922–1969) was one of the writers of the Beat Generation, a group that included such renowned figures as poet Allen Ginsberg (1926–1997) and novelist William Burroughs (1914–1997). Angelou recalls in *The Heart of a Woman* that Ginsberg was reading poetry in a coffeehouse next door to the nightclub where she was performing. Like him, she saw San Francisco as a proving ground for her talent.

On the Road is an explosive autobiographical novel about Kerouac's travels westward with Dean Moriarty (Neal Cassidy, 1926–1968), a fast driver and aspiring writer from Denver. *On the Road* became the supreme testimony to hip traveling in the 1950s. In *Heart of a Woman* Angelou compares the uncertainty of Kerouac's novel to life in America: Although we were traveling, we knew neither our "destination nor our arrival date" (3).

Thus, in these early pages, travel is connected to literary figures and uncertainty, to not knowing what is going to happen or when. The idea of indecision that Angelou so skillfully inserts into the beginning of her text diminishes as the story continues. As she moves from one setting to the next, staying nowhere for long and nowhere for certain, Angelou orchestrates the journey, moving the action back and forth in a spiral pattern with herself at the center. Like Noah, she has the stamina to stay afloat.

The journey outlined in *The Heart of a Woman* ends in the West African country of Ghana. Ghana marks the end of *All God's Children Need Traveling Shoes* as well. In these last two volumes, in spite of the geographical sweep of the narrative, Angelou has settled down, has moved from without to within. Although there is, as in the other texts, a narrative journey, the journey in *The Heart of a Woman* involves a voyage into the self as Angelou discovers the power of her language.

PLOT DEVELOPMENT

Unlike fictional forms such as the novel or the short story, the plot in autobiographies focuses on the revelation of character rather than on the development of a line of action. Further, the narrator of most autobiographies is more intent on exploring personal relationships than in plunging his/her characters into actions or escapades. Add these complications to the unusual, multilayered form of serial autobiography, with its mass of allusions to past situations, characters, and locations, and the nonplot thickens.

The plot in *The Heart of a Woman* has fewer emotional disruptions than in the three earlier autobiographies. Angelou performs in a more mature manner both as a mother and a professional. As an actress in Jean Genet's play *The Blacks* and as a political organizer in Martin Luther King's Southern Christian Leadership Conference, she achieves a level of competence not evident in the earlier volumes. *The Heart of a Woman* is the work that signals Angelou's maturity. She becomes more certain in her mothering, now that Guy is an adolescent. She promises herself to give up major tours, and finds fulfillment in her New York/Brooklyn environment—as an actress, a writer, and a political organizer.

Angelou's professional activities are interrupted when in 1961 she meets a South African, Vusumzi Make. At Vus's insistence they pretend they are married (133). The new husband goes to Cairo; Maya and Guy soon join him. The so-called marriage goes poorly, mainly because of money problems and Vus's promiscuity. The volume ends with Angelou and Vus divorced, and with mother and son en route to Liberia when Guy is seriously injured in a car accident.

CHARACTER DEVELOPMENT

Like all of the autobiographies in the series, *The Heart of a Woman* begins by creating a mood or an atmosphere into which the changing narrator is reintroduced. The fourth volume immediately places the story within a racial framework, with references to the military protection of Little Rock schoolchildren, to the blocking of a civil-rights bill by South Carolina Senator Strom Thurmond, and to other pertinent examples of the racist climate to which Angelou returns after a year in Europe performing in *Porgy and Bess*. As the story opens, she and Guy have moved from the security of Vivian Baxter's home to a houseboat near San Francisco that they share with four whites. Usually distrustful of white people, she is now, during the loose and free 1960s, part of an experimental gathering that she calls the "beatnik brigade." Her connection to her white roommates parallels her affinities with Kerouac, Ginsberg, and other liberated white writers of the 1950s.

However, Angelou is still somewhat distrustful and it shows through in indirect ways. She does not describe either her character or the characters of her roommates in a positive way; in fact, she barely describes them at all. In her remembrance of those "beatnik" days she provides the professions of her roommates—"an ichthyologist [a scientist who studies fish], a musician, a wife, and an inventor"(4)—and their race. But she never names or characterizes the people with whom she lives for almost a year, even though "naming" has been an important process in Angelou's writing, ever since Mrs. Cullinan so angers Maya by calling her Mary in *Caged Bird* that "Mary" deliberately breaks the nasty white woman's favorite casserole. As autobiographer, Angelou hastily bypasses the year on the houseboat, giving the impression that it was either too unpleasant, too embarrassing, or too trivial to recollect; it was, however, a necessary rite of passage in an era when the relationship between blacks and whites became looser, especially in large, "hip" areas like San Francisco.

While Angelou is not altogether satisfied with the integrated living situation and the communal structure of the houseboat, she is a long way from the experience of estrangement depicted at the beginning of her earlier volumes: the displaced and humiliated child of *I Know Why the Caged Bird Sings*, the guilty young mother of *Gather Together in My Name*, the lonely woman who sought refuge in music in *Singin' and Swingin' and Gettin' Merry Like Christmas*. On the houseboat she relaxes, becomes imaginative with her hairstyle and clothing. She particularly enjoys the experiment because her roommates neither ignore Maya's and Guy's skin color nor do they romanticize it. Angelou's brief stay in a commune reveals her capacity for cooperation and anticipates her later group involvements with writers, actors, and civil-rights workers.

Within a year, Angelou, tired of sharing space, craves privacy. She attempts, without initial success, to rent a small house in a segregated white neighborhood. The house, insists the landlord, is taken. Angelou seeks the help of some white friends, who pretend that the house is for them. Although the landlord finally concedes, the theme of racial discrimination is in the forefront during the early part of the book. At times, Angelou cheerfully coexists with white people, but at other times, as in the case of the landlord, she encounters prejudice similar to the episodes in *I Know Why the Caged Bird Sings*, when Dentist Lincoln refused to look into her mouth, or in *Gather Together in My Name*, when the saleswoman in Stamps insults her.

Similarly, Guy experiences racial discrimination from the staff of the white school he is attending. He is accused of using foul language in front of some girls on the school bus. When Angelou questions him, she learns that Guy rather tactlessly told them where babies come from. When he informed the innocent girls about their parents' role in making babies, they started to cry. Maya, who visits the school to discuss the problem, is once again confronted with racist attitudes; she is told that "we do not allow Negro boys to use foul language in front of our girls" (19). The teachers' attitudes were having a negative impact on her son.

Soon afterward mother and son move to a mixed neighborhood. Guy is overjoyed to see black children playing in the street. Maya becomes more relaxed in these circumstances. She begins to write sketches, songs, and stories. As luck has it, she meets African American novelist John Killens, who is in California writing a screenplay from one of his novels, *Youngblood*. Killens reads through her material, urging her to come to New York, where she will get feedback from other aspiring black writers.

The first dramatic change in Maya's character in *The Heart of a Woman* occurs when mother and son move to New York, where she and Guy live with John and Grace Killens and their family in Brooklyn until they find an apartment of their own. Guy is at first skeptical and disapproving, but they soon settle in—attending school, meeting neighbors, grappling with the differences they discover in leaving the West for the East. Angelou now seems confident in her lifestyle, her self-assurance deriving in part from the close relationships she is able to form with black singers, actors, and writers.

In the creative atmosphere of the East she starts to bloom, encouraged by talented African American friends and associates. It is not until this volume that Angelou, for the first time in the autobiography series, begins to identify herself as a writer. Readers can actually envision in this volume the distinguished artist who becomes the Maya Angelou of the 1990s.

Early on she mentions that she has begun to write sketches, songs, and short stories. In a marvelous episode, Angelou describes attending a workshop of the Harlem Writers Guild where she engages in a difficult procedure: a first reading of her only play, "One Love, One Life," followed by a none too flattering critique by the authors who attended. John Killens, trying to soften the blow to her writer's ego, tells her that the next time will be easier.

Determined to succeed, Angelou turns writing into an act of mental discipline. She forces herself to concentrate on details and to understand the technical aspects of the craft. Through the eventual encouragement that she receives from the Harlem Writer's Guild, she grows as a writer and as a person. She meshes her character with this group of African American and Caribbean writers more experienced than she, people who, like her, would someday make meaningful contributions to African American literature. John Killens, the member of the group most connected to Angelou's personal life, had at the time of their first meeting written *Youngblood* (1954), for which he was also writing the screenplay. Sarah Wright wrote the acclaimed novel *This Child's Gonna Live* (1969), a potent testimony to black female survival. Angelou's close friend, Rosa Guy, who protected her during stormy premarital clashes with Vus Make, was the author of *A Measure in Time* (1983) and other works of fiction. The Caribbean writer Paule Marshall—one of the most successful at the Harlem Writers Guild and now considered a major American novelist—was delighted to learn that her novel *Brown Girl, Brown Stones* (1959), was being made into a movie for television.

From reading *I Know Why the Caged Bird Sings*, readers know about Angelou's devotion to writers since childhood. Her earliest literary idols were men—James Weldon Johnson, Paul Lawrence Dunbar, and William Shakespeare. Although she admired women writers—Anne Spencer, Jessie Fauset, Nella Larsen, Zora Neale Hurston—she does not mention them in *Caged Bird* ("Icon" 1997). It is not until *The Heart of a Woman* that Angelou fully identifies herself with a woman writer. By taking that title from a poem by Georgia Douglas Johnson, she is including herself among a distinct tradition of women poets and novelists. Her allusion in the title to a caged black woman poet of the past is an acknowledgment to her legacy as a black woman writer, a legacy shared with Rosa Guy, Paule Marshall, and other sisters of African American and Caribbean ancestry.

These affiliations are indicative of Angelou's emerging feminism, which can be defined as a social and political response to the fact that women and men are treated unequally in society and that women are underrepresented in the arts, the sciences, the economy, and elsewhere. Angelou, in the acknowledgments to *The Heart of a Woman*, gives "Special thanks to a few of the many sister/friends whose love encourages me to spell my name: WOMAN." She then lists the names of twelve women whose friendships affected her sense of female identity, among them her friend of thirty years, Dolly A. McPherson; Ghanaian folklorist Efuah Sutherland; and novelists Rosa Guy, Paule Marshall, and Louise Merriwether.

Asked whether *The Heart of a Woman* is the book in which she starts becoming strongly identified as a woman writer rather than as someone whose connections are with male writers like Shakespeare or Poe, Angelou responded with a chuckle, "That's possible." "You can say that [in your book]. You can say anything you want," she said, again with a chuckle, displaying strength of character ("Icon" 1997).

In Harlem, Brooklyn, and Manhattan, Angelou takes advantage of opportunities for artistic improvement. She enters an apprenticeship with the Harlem Writers Guild and joins other African American organizations that sought the words and methods for creating a responsive, black-identified community. Like her work with the Writers Guild, Angelou's work in theater increases her potential for knowledge and friendship. She had good feelings from singing solo at Harlem's famous Apollo Theater and in other arenas attracting mainly black audiences. Her powerful renditions of Calypso music overjoy many of her listeners for whom Calypso and other types of folk songs are a neglected West Indian art form.

She is also successful in front of mixed or mainly white audiences, especially in her off-Broadway performance as the White Queen in the 1961 production of Jean Genet's 1961 play *The Blacks*. Genet's infamous play is a vicious satire about the absurdity of white racism. In the play, the black/white roles are reversed so that the formerly oppressed blacks become the aggressors and the formerly affluent whites become their pawns. Angelou loves playing the leading role, even though the idea of reversal of power does not appeal to her sense of democracy. She is particularly fond of one of the actors in the cast, Godfrey Cambridge, who in 1970, the year *Caged Bird* is published, performs his memorable role as *Watermelon Man*, directed by Melvin Van Peebles which, like *The Blacks*, is a drama based on role reversal.

Angelou and Cambridge, swayed by the ideas of Martin Luther King Jr. collaborate on a fund-raising project at the Village Gate, a popular night club in Grenwich Village, to benefit the Southern Christian Leadership Conference. Called Cabaret for Freedom, the fund-raiser is created, directed, and performed by Angelou and Cambridge, with help from comics, dancers, and other theater people. Yet despite the cabaret project and a developing personal friendship, Angelou and Cambridge never become lovers. Between them, Angelou says, they "ignited no passionate fires" (53).

A far more public person than she was in the earlier volumes, Angelou begins to identify with the emerging civil-rights movement after working on the fund-raiser. Eventually she becomes Northern Coordinator of the Southern Christian Leadership Conference (SCLC). She is also committed to a women's organization, the Cultural Association for Women of African Heritage (CAWAH).

Soon after meeting South African hero Vusumzi Make in 1961, Angelou and the women of CAWAH almost halt the operations of the UN General Assembly when they conduct a sit-in at the United Nations Building after the Prime Minister of Zaire, Patrice Lumumba is assassinated in 1961. To assist their cause, Angelou and her friend Rosa Guy seek out the support of Black Muslim leader Malcolm X. She and Rosa hope that he and his organization will affirm the actions of CAWAH and make use of the energy incited by the protest gathering. To the contrary, Malcolm X is very disapproving of the protest strategy: "Muslims do not demonstrate," he responded (168). Although he predicts that conservative African American leaders, wanting to be loved by the white man, will quickly turn against the organizers, he does offer to tell the press that the protest means black people are angry. Angelou, although she is disappointed with Malcolm X's response, is nonetheless entranced by his good looks and his fire, traits that had also attracted her to South African rebel Vusumzi Make.

The second major change in Angelou's character occurs when she meets Vusumzi Make, a freedom fighter recently released from a South African prison. They meet at a party given by John Killens and his wife to protest apartheid in South Africa, the systematic and total segregation of South African people into two groups: the privileged whites and the disenfranchised blacks. In her book of reflective essays, *Even the Stars Look Lonesome* (1997), Angelou describes Vus Make as one of the most brilliant people she had ever met.

A handsome, dazzling intellectual, Vus Make appears to be the perfect choice for a husband, given Maya's desire to be loved and her growing concern for African liberation movements. Angelou is already engaged to a bailbondsman, Thomas Allen, a smooth man of "reddish-tan color" who gives her "lavish satisfaction" (100). But Vus is electrifying, exciting, beautiful; if she marries Thomas she would always regret her decision. Vus and Maya go through the motions of marrying in England. Vus suggested as a formality that in America they claim to have married in England, while in London they say their marriage took place in New York: "We never mentioned the word marriage again" (133).

But in London the couple soon begins to spend less time together. Through her husband, Maya starts to associate with a community of middle-class African women who warn her that marriage to an African freedom fighter can often lead to desertion. As Maya listens to her sisters' stories about their struggles under colonialism, she enthralls them with heroic tales about African American women. With great pride Angelou tells of Harriet Tubman, who, though free, returned to the South to bring slaves out of bondage, and of Sojourner Truth, who had the courage to speak for the rights of enslaved blacks even though white leaders denied that she was a woman and a human being.

As Vus continues to neglect her, Angelou again proves herself vulnerable to male authority, as she was with Curly, L. D. Tolbrook, Tosh Angelos, and other men in her past. In her role as Vus's wife, she is confronted for the second time with the struggle between being a home-maker and being a professional, as she had struggled in earlier autobiographies between being a mother and being a professional. As an African who had been trained only to see women as subservient, Vus Make is culturally insensitive to Angelou's needs as a working woman.

In one hilarious sequence that occurs before they are a couple, Angelou accompanies Vus to a cocktail party in the Manhattan suite of a West African ambassador. Although she is wearing her most flattering dress and can speak fluently about international politics in several languages, the guests ignore her because she is an American woman. Maya's way out of this embarrassment is to sit in the kitchen drinking gin with the black female cook. When Vus discovers her, he is humiliated and furious: "No African lady would bring such disgrace on her husband" (203). He chases the now drunken Maya around the lobby of the classy building where she eludes him, grabs a cab out from under the nose of a waiting woman, and spends the night with her friend, novelist Rosa Guy.

If Vus could be so uncompromising in New York, readers can imagine his attitude when they move to Cairo. He expects Angelou to honor the Egyptian custom of the husband providing for the wife. Nonetheless, Angelou accepts a position as associate editor with the *Arab Observer* without getting Vus's permission. In a torrent of fury, he reproaches her, suggesting that she is a man. All is chaos until a mutual friend and American journalist, David DuBois, persuades Vus that her salary will help them serve the revolutionary cause.

Nor is the conflict between wife and freedom worker the only trouble in the union. Years later, Angelou confided that her formerly passionate lover had a "startling intellect and an impressive accumulation of information, but was shy a mile from romance" (*Stars* 55). She begins to realize—as she knew very well from his behavior while they were in America—that Vus Make is too friendly with other women and too irresponsible with money. Their irreconcilable positions toward fidelity and financial commitment require that they be examined in a palaver, an Egyptian debate conducted among peers from six countries and intended to clarify the opposing positions with regard to separation. The tribunal decides in Maya's favor but asks her to stay with Vus for six more months. She agrees, but when there is a job offer from Liberia in West Africa, she accepts it.

Angelou's disastrous relationship with Vusumzi Make evokes certain comparisons and contrasts to her marriage to Tosh Angelos in *Singin' and Swingin'*. Further retracing Angelou's steps, the first pages of *Caged Bird* recall the failed marriage between Bailey Johnson Sr. and Vivian Baxter, with its negative impact on Angelou's life as a child and a woman. In the course of her life, Angelou introduces problems or conditions that echo other volumes, giving them unity or offering points of contrast. This technique can be called connective repetition, a term Angelou seems to distrust, insisting that each book must stand alone. While each book in a serial autobiography must be read independently, the reading process is greatly enriched by recognizing subtle references in and among the texts. The modifications in plot, character, and setting that are bound to occur in serial autobiographies benefit from being examined for their interrelated moments, and in Angelou's case, emphasis on her diverging attitudes toward her autobiographical self.

The most valuable aspect of her relationship with Vus Make is its connection to her growing romance with Africa. In the fourth and fifth volumes, Africa is the site of her growth—first in Cairo, the capital of Egypt, and then in Accra, the capital of Ghana. In these tightly interrelated volumes, Angelou initiates a search for her ancestral past. A developing writer, her continuing identification with language and character makes her sensitive to her African roots. She begins to articulate her connections to African slaves who had been "shackled with chains," and made to carry the weight of their fears with the weight of their irons (257). Her racial consciousness becomes a major theme in *All God's Children Need Traveling Shoes* in which she explores her feelings of guilt about slavery and about being homeless, neither an African nor an African American. Her search does not culminate until the struggle of her dual ancestry is resolved.

Near the end of *The Heart of a Woman*, Maya meets her greatest challenge when Guy's car is hit by a truck outside of Accra. An old couple found him on the road and brought him to the emergency ward. At the hospital while her son lies on a stretcher, Maya contemplates his "rich golden skin" turned to "ash-grey" (263). Angelou, although she rarely repeats the same episode in detail, does so in this instance, restating many of the aspects of Guy's accident at the beginning of her next book, *All God's Children Need Traveling Shoes*.

The deliberate repetition of her terror creates both an emotional link between the two volumes and underscores the impact of Guy's injuries on both character and story line, since it is Guy's car crash that keeps Angelou in Ghana. Her retelling of the car accident, first in volume 4 and again in volume 5, emphasizes the autobiographical experience and the use of the mother/son theme as a transitional device. When asked about the repetition of the car crash, Angelou said she repeated the scene because she had to explain where she was and why, so that each book would be read in its own right ("Icon" 1997). In terms of dramatic effect, the startling repetition gives the volumes an intensity not achieved anywhere else in the series.

As in *Singin' and Swingin' and Gettin' Merry Like Christmas*, in *The Heart of a Woman* Angelou remains in a state of flux, continuously open to changes in her life, even when those changes involve her divorce from Vus Make and her suffering over her injured son. As she faces these problems she continues the process of redefining her self. In *The Heart of a Woman* Angelou's more stable character derives from the self-assurance that comes from long years of living and mothering, her success with writing, and her engagement in theatre and politics. Angelou's self-assurance, hinted at in earlier volumes, is heightened in *The Heart of a Woman*, becoming a major aspect of her character.

SETTING

In the fourth volume the setting pivots from a western to a distinctively eastern environment. The volume has three primary settings—San Francisco, New York, and Egypt. These disparate settings divide the book in three parts, with New York placed in the middle or central location. In San Francisco Maya solidifies her relationship with Guy and lovingly ends her dependency on Vivian Baxter. In New York she achieves greater self-awareness as mother and, through the Harlem Writers Guild, explores her potential as a writer. In Cairo she introduces herself to the idea of what it means to be African as she struggles to maintain her relationship with Vus Make. The primary locations in *The Heart of a Woman* affect Maya's growth in terms of motherhood, the black literary scene, and her African heritage.

Secondary settings, places visited for short durations, also have strong effects on character development and plot. In the London sequence, for example, Maya accompanies Vus Make to England, where they had planned to get married. Maya is intrigued by the cosmopolitan setting of London; she enjoys the contrasts—the bright costumes of African women reflected against the stony grayness of London. The city also connects her to a support group of women living in London and married to African officials. London with Vus offers another type of newness for Maya as she encounters the sensual ecstasy of making love with a dazzling, delightful male.

Angelou's most dramatic use of setting occurs near the end of *The Heart of a Woman*. In prose that creates the effect of cinemascope or Imax, she offers a panoramic view of North Africa as she flies from Cairo in the east to Ghana in the west, reversing the earlier west/east movement from San Francisco to New York. She gazes from the plane and sees the Sahara desert, then the rivers and forests where she imagines children had been hunted and "tethered" by slave traders. Her vision projects her to America, where she traces the black American's unending "journey to misery," to the outrages of slavery (257). Angelou registers some of the major themes of *The Heart of a Woman* in this secondary setting as she is propelled across the continent: compassion, the journey, the identification with slavery. The African setting continues in the volume that follows, *All God's Children Need Traveling Shoes*.

THEMATIC ISSUES

Motherhood, so dominant a theme in each of the autobiographies, takes on a new complexity in *The Heart of a Woman*, owing to the presence and absence of Maya's mother, Vivian Baxter. The complications of the motherhood theme, can be demonstrated by dividing it into three different issues: Maya mothering Guy; Vivian mothering Maya mothering Vivian; and Maya mothering herself.

In the opening sequences of the book, Maya defends Guy on two different occasions when he is accused of misconduct at school. She also tries to protect him against the outrageous tirades of blues singer Billie Holiday. As she gets ready to leave for New York, Angelou observes that her son is changing, that he is, at the age of fourteen, "growing into a tall aloof stranger" (22).

Despite his aloofness, Guy and his mother remain close throughout

The Heart of a Woman. On one level, she improves in her ability to care for him and solicit his opinions; on another, she continues the persistent problem of separation begun in *Gather Together* and *Singin' and Swingin'* when she loses touch with his life and needs.

The best example in volume 4 of Angelou's conflict with motherhood occurs in the episode involving the Brooklyn gang, the Savages. It is highlighted by the fact that when Guy gets in trouble with the gang Angelou is in Chicago on a singing engagement. One night, John Killens, who is watching over Guy while she is away, phones from Brooklyn to inform her that "there's been some trouble" (75). In a moment of fear, Angelou imagines that Guy has been injured and that it has somehow been her fault. She chastises herself for being a "capricious and too-often-absent mother" (106). She has not been responsible enough.

The motif of the responsible mother occurs frequently in the series. In *Gather Together*, she travels alone on a long bus ride to confront Big Mary Dalton, who had kidnapped Guy. In an early incident in *The Heart of a Woman* she looks three white schoolteachers in the eye when they accuse Guy of upsetting some little girls. The Brooklyn gang event is also the result of a girl accusing Guy: the gang-leader's girlfriend claims that Guy hit her. Knowing the passions of teenagers, Angelou takes extreme measures to protect her son. When she confronts Jerry, the gang leader, she threatens to shoot his entire family if anything happens to Guy. She has a gun in her purse to prove it.

The confrontation with Jerry reveals Angelou as a strong, aggressive, perhaps too impulsive black mother who puts aside her guilt and self-doubt in order to defend her son. She said, in an interview: "I've always been adventurous or up to life. Even not adventurous, but when life says 'Here you are, deal with it,' I have dealt with it, or tried to" ("Icon" 1997). Defiant, protective of Guy and his welfare, Angelou becomes in this episode a representation of maternal power. In her dealings with the street gang, Angelou embodies a type of black woman whom Joanne M. Braxton calls the "outraged mother" (1989, 21). This type, claims Braxton, is found frequently in slave narratives by women; she represents the strength and dedication of the black mother.

With regard to her own mother, Vivian Baxter, Maya makes a special effort to say "good bye" as she ends a long and complicated relationship. When she knows that she is leaving California, Maya contacts her mother and requests a formal farewell. Vivian Baxter, always defiant, always ready for an adventure, tells her daughter to meet her for an overnight visit at the Desert Hotel in Fresno. The Desert Hotel had been integrated for only a month, so when Maya meets Vivian in the lounge she feels as though she is about to be stabbed or at least lassoed. Vivian, cool as usual, flirts with the bartender; Maya stares at her mother and repeats the observation from *Caged Bird* that she was "the most beautiful woman I had ever seen" (25). When they get to their room Vivian shows her the gun in her purse, the possible inspiration for Maya's gun in her future confrontation with Jerry.

In this scene, Angelou reveals that she is still enthralled by the beautiful woman from St. Louis, the woman "too beautiful to have children" (*Caged Bird* 50). She has since come to appreciate her mother for her vibrant sexuality and her free spirit. Forty years after their rendezvous in Fresno, Vivian Baxter, no longer "beautiful," will be at Maya's house in North Carolina, her arms stuck with tubes, spending her last days fighting cancer in her daughter's care. "My mother raised me, then freed me," Angelou writes (*Stars* 48). It is now time to free her mother.

Toward the end of *The Heart of a Woman* a mature Maya Angelou finds herself increasingly alone. The relationship with Vus Make is over. Vivian is in California. Guy, gradually recovering from his physical injuries, moves toward greater autonomy. As the volume ends, he has moved into a university dormitory and she is alone. In the last two paragraphs, Angelou is by herself, testing her independence from Guy as she had earlier in the narrative tested her independence from Vus Make. Despite Guy's absence or perhaps because of it, she recognizes an emerging new self, a woman liberated in heart and being. The last word of *The Heart of a Woman* is "myself."

The narrator's singular aloneness in this final scene is superficially concerned with what she is eating. No longer needing to compete with her son over who gets the best part of the chicken, she has the breast all to herself without having to share it. There is significant irony here. As Angelou has so often resorted to humor when faced with a disturbing problem, in the conclusion of the fourth volume she offers the reader the half-serious picture of a greedy mother getting what she has always wanted. Her keeping the breast represents both the nurturing aspect of the mother as well as a weaning herself from Guy's demands. Life for Angelou, whether she wants it to or not, is about to offer a new freedom, a new character, a new "myself." No longer the mother saved from drugs at the close of *Gather Together* or the mother prone to making false promises in *Singin' and Swingin'*, the character at the end of *The Heart of a Woman* is, as the title states, a woman. Defined as neither mother nor wife, Maya Angelou is at this moment simply herself.

STYLE AND LITERARY DEVICES

Of the many stylistic techniques that recur in *The Heart of a Woman*, two in particular give the volume its special power: the dynamic portrait and the literary allusion. Although Angelou uses the technique of portraiture in all of the volumes, it is not until the fourth autobiography that she perfects it. This device is also called a descriptive portrait or vignette.

The vignette in literature is a leisurely, ornamental description used to depict character, a technique especially appropriate to autobiography, which lacks the plot-driven intensity of a novel. A realistic way to introduce character is through brief descriptive portraits and the more full-blown vignette. Exciting but short descriptions of celebrities include Angelou's references to musicians Max Roach and Abbey Lincoln, writers James Baldwin and Lorraine Hansberry, Martin Luther King, Jr. and other prominent African Americans. These portraits strengthen the development of Angelou's story by introducing figures of great interest who are subordinate to the main events of the narrative. Intertwined with the text, the characters mainly please readers because they are interesting people.

The second, more complex portrait (or vignette) relies on compactness of style in offering a condensed description designed to capture the subject's mannerisms and quirks as well as leave a lasting impression on readers. At their most successful, Angelou's vignettes are character studies of famous African Americans who emerge as intensely realized characters, people who, because of her involvement in show business and politics, Angelou has had the chance to scrutinize. Men or women whom readers may have admired from afar—from a platform, stage, or pulpit—are drawn so near that Angelou is able to expose their wit, imperfections, nastiness, and benevolence.

In *The Heart of a Woman*, the two most notable vignettes are of Billie Holiday and Malcolm X. For a period of four days, Maya Angelou entertains blues singer Billie Holiday in California. Their meeting occurs a few months before Holiday's death in a New York hospital. Angelou harshly describes how drugs destroyed the singer's beautiful face: her eyes were blank, her skin rubbery. In her description of their four-day friendship, Angelou captures Lady Day's moody anger, her vivid language, her unpredictable shifts of mood.

Guy is greatly disturbed by Billie's presence in the house. He constantly chatters at her, as if to fill the air. Each night she sings him a bedtime song. On her last night, as she is singing "Strange Fruit," a heartbreaking song about a lynching, Guy keeps interrupting her with questions. Enraged, Holiday tells Guy that the crackers will cut off the balls of a "little nigger" like him (14).

Later that evening, Maya is singing at a club and realizes that Billie is in the audience. After Maya announces her presence, Holiday takes an unsmiling bow from her table. Then, as Maya starts singing a blues song, Lady Day screams: "Stop that bitch. She sounds just like my goddam Momma" (15). Holiday's actions, so disturbing to Maya and her son, are discussed further in the Psychological/Feminist Reading section at the end of this chapter.

The other vignette that stands out in *The Heart of a Woman* is the portrait of Malcolm X, whose brief but intense characterization tells us a great deal about Angelou's eroticism. She describes this remote Muslim leader in the language of desire. Maya Angelou and Rosa Guy have made an appointment with Malcolm X to request Muslim support for the CAWAH rally at the United Nations. When he enters the meeting place it feels to Maya as if a "hot desert storm" is rushing at her. His "masculine force" overwhelms her; he was "a great arch through which one could pass to eternity" (167). Angelou's breathless seizure is almost like being physically invaded, and by a man whose political control and personal dignity do nothing to encourage her fantasies of burning hair and blazing eyes.

Angelou handles the remainder of the vignette in a cooler manner. Malcolm X describes at some length the teachings of the Honorable Elijah Muhammad on the need to separate from white men and their false Christianity, for they have enslaved the African. He promises to offer the people of Harlem the Muslim religion. And he promises to make a statement to the press saying that the protest at the UN Building was a sign of the anger of black people.

Angelou's dramatic use of the vignette as a way of characterizing Malcolm X works well in this case, for it is both a portrait and a sermon, a lesson from the great Muslim leader that helps teach her something about self-respect and self-control. Her use of Malcolm X's portrait as a stylistic device continues into the fifth volume, *All God's Children Need Traveling Shoes*, where he is again singled out in a vignette.

The second distinctive stylistic technique in *The Heart of a Woman* is the literary allusion, which Meyer H. Abrams explains as a "reference, without explicit identification, to a person, place, or event, or to another literary work or passage" (8). Angelou enriches her text by connecting it to significant people and places within African American traditions. This discussion focuses on one specific literary allusion—to the Georgia Douglas Johnson poem for which *The Heart of a Woman* is named.

Earlier in this chapter the influence of Georgia Douglas Johnson and other African American women on Angelou's writing was discussed. At the heart of Johnson's poem, "Heart of a Woman" (1927), there is a continuing metaphor that spans several volumes in the autobiographies: It is the comparison between the first-person narrator and the caged bird. The bird/poet comparison begins when Angelou borrowed the title, *I Know Why the Caged Bird Sings*, from Paul Lawrence Dunbar's poem, "Sympathy." Dunbar's caged bird is generally associated with the condition of black people in America who are imprisoned by whites when they desire to be free. In her sketches of Uncle Willie, Bailey, and other characters, Angelou occasionally uses images of imprisonment, suggesting, like Dunbar, that blacks survive being caged by turning to their culture for strength.

Johnson's "The Heart of a Woman" is an eight-line lyric poem in which a woman's heart is compared to a caged bird crashing against its bars. Johnson's use of the symbol of the bird, however, is quite different from Dunbar's, for her bird is a caged woman whose isolation seems to suggest sexual rather than racial confinement. Like a bird, the heart of a woman flies away from home during the day, returning at night to its cage.

Because both Georgia Douglas Johnson and Maya Angelou deal with the theme of isolation and because both use the metaphor of the caged bird in their writings, it is tempting to view Angelou's allusion to Johnson's trapped bird as a negative reference to Maya's character in *The Heart of a Woman*. James Robert Saunders (1991), for example, states that the "alien cage" of Johnson's poem represents Angelou's return to a place of torment following her failed marriage to Vus Make. It seems that Angelou, with her awareness of black history and literature, would have regarded Johnson's lonely bird in flight as a stage in a woman's life cycle and in her history. The Douglas poem was written in 1927, only seven years after the passing of the 19th amendment to the U.S. Constitution, on August 26, 1920, which finally granted women the right to vote. Angelou, while facing barriers of race and gender, has flown beyond them, thanks to the very protest movements described in the fourth autobiography. The broken creature of Johnson's 1927 poem is an image from the past, too forlorn to symbolize Angelou's failed marriage. Although she may indeed sympathize with the sad prisoner of Johnson's lyric, the Maya Angelou of *The Heart of a Woman* is too strong and too self-determined to be kept in a cage.

Angelou's *The Heart of a Woman* also contains other literary allusions. The opening reference to Jack Kerouac's *On the Road* connects Angelou's theme of the journey to Kerouac's restlessness. Angelou makes reference to the black folk figure, Brer Rabbit, in a story she recalls to herself in Cairo as she gathers courage for her new job on the *Arab Observer*. Her use of Brer Rabbit connects her to the oral traditions of Africa and America. But it is in the allusion to Johnson's title, to the repeated "WOMAN" of both poem and autobiography, that one discovers a more woman-centered Maya Angelou—more centered in her literary ambitions, more centered in her racial identity.

A PSYCHOLOGICAL/FEMINIST READING

Psychological criticism is the application of the beliefs of Sigmund Freud, Otto Rank, Karen Horney, and other psychological theorists to works of literature, in the hopes of getting closer to their meaning. In a standard psychological reading of *The Heart of a Woman*, theorists begin by investigating Guy's relationship to his mother or to a mother sub-stitute. A number of incidents reveal Guy's sexual desire for women his mother's age or older, the most prominent of which is for Billie Holi-day. The great blues singer, who seems to disgust Guy, also arouses him. During her visit, Holiday sings intimately to Guy each night, giving Maya the impression that Holiday was "starved for sex and only the boy, looking at her out of bored young eyes, could give her satisfaction" (13).

A Freudian analyst argues that in order to free himself from his Oed-ipus complex—the desire to dispose of the father and have sex with the mother—Guy needed to deflect Holiday's affections away from himself and his mother, just as he needed to discourage Maya's affair to Vus Make. Not until Guy experienced and recovered from his car accident could he begin to sever himself from his desirable mother, who, accord-ing to his friends, has "a prettier shape than Marilyn Monroe" (130). Some far-fetched analyst might even suggest that the accident was "in-tentional," that Guy desired it so he could be saved from his sexual desires for his mother.

In a psychological/feminist reading, it is not the boy's or the man's perspective that one starts with but the woman's. Many feminists find the "Oedipus complex," the so-called cornerstone of Freudian thinking, to be utterly wrong-headed, since the theory assumes that the mother is of no consequence and that she is subordinate to the father or the father substitute (Stanton in Wright 1992, 296). In the 1970s a number of feminist analysts, including Nancy Chodorov, Carol Gilligan, and Jean Baker Miller, challenged this male way of thinking. In their revision of psychological theory they proposed a woman-oriented perspective, focusing on the ideas that the mother is central to human development; that mother/daughter relationships are at the core of development; and that female friendships can be extensions of the mother/daughter dynamic to the extent that they are nurturing, supportive, and maternal.

The Heart of a Woman offers a wealth of woman-centered insights. As a woman who loves men, Angelou is very open about her sexual feelings, making almost no effort to conceal her inclinations. She craves sex, but she likes being satisfied. She is neither passive nor timid in approaching men. She is in her words a "healthy woman with a healthy appetite" (101).

Angelou also appears to be a woman who is enticed by women, although she tends to deny this possibility, both in the autobiographies and in public statements. In the crucial Billie Holiday sequence in *The Heart of a Woman*, Maya protests against the possibility of Holiday's lesbianism, working out a careful negative response so that if Billie wants to go to bed with her, Maya can say no without hurting her feelings. A psychological feminist would help Angelou deal with her conflicting attitudes towards lesbianism, suggesting a greater openness toward the likelihood that she consciously or unconsciously desires women more than she is willing to admit.

Moving to safer but surely related grounds, it was in the 1970s that psychological feminists began to suggest that lesbianism was most likely connected to the relationship between mother and daughter. The positive treatment of the mother/daughter relationship was another area of analysis that had been almost completely overlooked until the coming of the Women's Movement. Looking to her childhood, it is likely that Angelou's complex range of feelings toward women was based on the absence of her mother at the age of three, the age that so-called Oedipal feelings are considered to be most critical. When at age eight Maya is again reunited with Vivian Baxter, she is raped by her mother's boyfriend, a rather obvious father figure. Unable to deal with the sexual life of her daughter, Vivian sends her back to her grandmother, not becoming close to Maya until the child/woman is sixteen. All of these circumstances generate conflicting attitudes toward being a woman.

In *The Heart of a Woman* the most passionate parts of the book have to do with Billie Holiday and Vivian Baxter. These relationships, as well as a number of others involving both men and women, depend on Maya's early experiences with her mother, which include abandonment; feelings of rejection; feelings of being ugly when compared to the beautiful Vivian; exposure to a rapist. Each of these areas is open to feminist discourse. A committed and knowledgeable psychological feminist reading could continue to expand on Angelou's feelings about being a woman, analyzing them in *The Heart of a Woman* and in the entire autobiographical series.

All God's Children Need Traveling Shoes
(1986)

The fifth volume of Maya Angelou's autobiography, *All God's Children Need Traveling Shoes*, tells the story of Angelou's four-year residency in Ghana from 1963 to 1966. When the narrative was published twenty years later, it was greeted with praise and disappointment. Eugenia Collier, on the one hand, proclaimed the book to be "the apex toward which the other autobiographies have pointed" (1986, 24), while Russell Harris, on the other hand, told Angelou the book was too "pedantic," too academic. Except for the quest idea, there was not much of a story line. She replied: "I think you might need another reading, because there are other stories in the book" (1989, 168).

One major story found in *Traveling Shoes*, one that most critics overlook, is Angelou's love for her son. The volume begins with a reiteration of Guy's car accident, the episode that concluded *The Heart of a Woman*. In *Traveling Shoes* Guy recovers from his injuries and continues to mature. A student at the University of Ghana, he seeks independence from his mother as he attempts to define his own separate goals.

Another major story is Angelou's exploration of her African and African American identities. She explores this conflict as it exists for the American expatriates living in Accra as well as for the groups of people—Bambara, Keta, Ahanta—who still observe the traditions of their ancestors. At the end of *Traveling Shoes* these issues are resolved when Angelou decides to return to the ways and culture of the United States.

Surrounded by friends at the Accra airport, she leaves Guy in Africa to
finish his education. At the same time she forsakes her newly embraced
alliance with Mother Africa, claiming she is "not sad" to be leaving
Ghana (209).

NARRATIVE POINT OF VIEW AND STRUCTURE

The narrative point of view in *All God's Children Need Traveling Shoes*
is again sustained through the first-person autobiographer in motion. She
moves from journey to journey, propelling the story from one place to
another. It is not accidental that the word *traveling* appears in the title.
The autobiography begins with Maya's and Guy's travel to Ghana and
ends with her anticipated departure to America in the concluding lines
of the autobiography. Told from the first-person point of view, the fifth
volume, like the others, is subjective. Owing perhaps to the dominance
of the travel motif, it is at the same time more tightly controlled.

In *All God's Children Need Traveling Shoes*, the African narrative is interrupted by a journey within a journey. Angelou accepts the offer to
join a theatrical company in a revival of French writer Jean Genet's play
The Blacks. Three years earlier *The Blacks* shocked its off-Broadway audiences with the force of its racial commentary. In that performance,
described in *The Heart of a Woman*, Angelou triumphed in the sinister
role of the White Queen. Now the play was being revived, and Angelou
was asked to repeat the role on a limited tour, with performances in
Berlin and Venice. The consequences of the Berlin journey are analyzed
later in this chapter, in the sections on setting and character. In terms of
point of view, the German sequence offers a glimpse of Angelou as traveler in an alien land with a history of racial prejudice quite different
from what she experienced in America.

As in all her volumes, the title contributes to the plot and to the thematic impact. Angelou states that the title of the fifth volume comes from
a spiritual about walking in Heaven: "I've got shoes / you got shoes /
All of God's children got shoes" ("Icon" 1997). The traveling shoes that
belong to the narrator and to all children of African descent restate the
journey motif. As she told George Plimpton, the book is about "trying
to get home," which for Jews would mean Israel and for black Americans
would mean Africa (1990, rpt. 1994, 20).

On a much lighter note, the traveling shoes might also refer to the pair
of feet made famous by writer Langston Hughes in his *Best of Simple*:

"These feet have walked ten thousand miles working for white folks and another ten thousand keeping up with colored" (1989, 100). In his amusing way, in this story about Simple's weary feet, Hughes suggests the long stretch of unwanted travel taken by African Americans in the last century of so-called freedom. Angelou speaks passionately of Hughes in *Caged Bird* as an example of the "wit and humor" that he shares with Dorothy Parker and Edna St. Vincent Millay (and with Angelou herself) ("Icon" 1997).

SETTING

Setting or place, always an important element in Angelou's writing, assumes its greatest prominence in the fifth volume. Most of the action is set in Accra, the capital of the West African nation of Ghana. The minute details of contemporary African life, contrasted against ancient customs, lend the volume an exotic backdrop from which to view personal events like Guy's recovery from the car crash or Maya's feelings of dislocation. The African setting plays an important, almost inseparable part in her character development.

Additionally, in presenting the African setting as a major component of the fifth autobiography, Angelou, like other writers before her, describes to an American readership her impressions of what white explorers once called the Dark Continent, *dark* suggesting to them Africa's quality of mystery as well as the dark complexion of most of her people. In the first sentence of *Traveling Shoes* she describes the secret night breezes and how they vanish into the "utter blackness." Angelou is often intrigued by blackness, and in one of the most passionate moments of a February 1996, interview on *Lifetime* television, she begins to praise the dark skin of Mrs. Flowers, her mentor in *I Know Why the Caged Bird Sings*, simultaneously stroking her own face in a recognition of black pride. As described in *Traveling Shoes*, the dark skin colors of the Ghanaians remind her of peanut butter, caramel, and other treats from childhood. She admires Sheikhali, her suitor from Mali, for the purple hues of his skin; her beautician, Comfort Adday, for being the color of "ancient bricks" (37); and her roommate Alice Windom for her "dark, mahogany color" (30). The interaction of skin tones with clothing and landscape contributes significantly to the unfolding of character and setting.

Further settings on the periphery of the African locale are Berlin and Venice, the two cities she visits as the White Queen in the revival of *The*

Blacks. Although Angelou's inclusion of the Berlin-Venice tour might be viewed as a digression that detracts from the African-based setting, the theater sequence helps contribute to her character development and, through use of contrast, to the profound exploration of her feelings for a homeland. The Berlin setting offers Angelou an unusual perspective. She is remote enough from Africa to gain new insights into the behavior of black Americans and the nature of white racism, both reflected against the German terrain. She gains a new respect for African Americans, missing them now because they seem more spirited than the Africans she has encountered in Ghana. These interruptions in the Ghanaian setting are effective in giving *Traveling Shoes* a universal quality as the autobiographer reaches beyond her private life into a conflicting world.

PLOT DEVELOPMENT

In terms of plot development, *Traveling Shoes* is consistent with the earlier volumes. Each is designed to be a continuing journey of the self. The plot of *Traveling Shoes* begins in Ghana and terminates with Angelou's decision to return to America, thus ending both the series and the journey. She leaves for conscious reasons involving her heritage, her craft, and her private life, especially as it relates to her son.

Angelou's autobiographies receive their shape from personal and cultural referents rather than from the necessities of plot, as in mystery novels or spy fiction. Whereas a novel is a kind of narrative that must be concluded, an autobiography is an unfinished narrative, told in the first person by the adult who recollects it years later. *All God's Children Need Traveling Shoes* cannot conclude the series because there are potentially more autobiographies to be written, from images and actions that remain in the repository of memories that connect her to the people around her.

Soon after volume 5 opens, the narrator, now thirty-three, relates the horrifying event of Guy's car accident that results in a broken arm, leg, and neck. When asked why she repeated the accident scene, which also ends *The Heart of a Woman*, Angelou gave two reasons: First, each book must stand alone; and, second, it was necessary that she explain who she was and what she was doing in Africa ("Icon" 1997).

In order to infuse the African setting with a credible plot, Angelou needed to detail the causes for her lengthy stay. She intensifies the early pages by dramatizing her long wait for medical reports from a hospital totally foreign to her. Many parents' greatest fear is the death of a child; this is the most unspeakable of all catastrophes. Angelou universalizes this fear in *Traveling Shoes*, taking readers close to death but then reversing the expectation. Readers, raised on popular melodrama, expect Guy to die and Angelou to fall apart. But true to her point of view, Angelou elucidates the slow pain of Guy's recovery. There is no catastrophe. As time passes, he gradually moves out of danger and regains his strength. Simultaneously, Maya demonstrates her increased maturity. Like most people whose children grow up, she starts to appreciate her freedom now that the burdens and responsibilities of motherhood are lessened. Aware that she must respect Guy's choices, she consciously ceases to make him the center of her activities. She forms new friendships—with her roommates, African poets, African American writers and artists living in Ghana.

At the same time, Angelou strengthens her ties with Mother Africa. In traveling through eastern Ghana, she forms allegiances with people she meets and also becomes spiritually attached to her venerated ancestors. These intimate racial, political, and sacred connections with Africans allow Angelou to recognize but not resolve the dual nature of her heritage. By the end of *Traveling Shoes* she has explored her roots, has come to terms with much of her past, and has decided to return to America to begin a new phase of her life, one that assimilates the African and American elements of her character: "I think in *All God's Children* I have written about some of the complexity of returning, at one, and being unable to return [to Africa] and yet being so grateful that I had made the attempt" ("Icon" 1997).

The mother/son plot, like the African/African American plot, is dual in nature. To develop the plot is to create a series of active/counteractive rhythms. The confrontations between love and desertion, between knowledge and misunderstanding, are two examples of the shifting story that shape the series.

For Angelou, though, the termination of plot seems less successful here than in her other volumes, possibly because she forces her narrator/self to present too sharp a separation between herself and Africa. Four years earlier, African American novelist Alice Walker attempted in *The Color Purple* (1982) to unify similar geographical (Africa/America) and familial (Sister Celie/Sister Nattie) themes. At the end of the novel, Nettie arrives from Africa with her husband, Samuel, their two children, Olivia and Adam, and a young African woman, Tashi, who is Adam's wife. Everyone has come, united at last in one colossal family reunion. But Walker's finale is too perfect, too out of place in a novel that so consistently raised the questions of race and gender in America. Director Steven Spielberg, in his 1985 film version of *The Color Purple*, ignored many of the book's socio-economic issues but retained Walker's joyous resolution, visually amplified through the use of dazzling African costumes and children's clapping games.

Like Walker, Maya Angelou attempts to tie together the divergent strands that inform the fifth autobiography. Thus, the final scene at the Accra airport is crowded with a farewell contingent of sages, poets, ex-patriates, dancers, dignitaries, college students, professors, and children. But as John C. Gruesser points out, the end of Angelou's journey is not convincing. The conflicts inherent in the book remain unresolved and the ending is "too easily manufactured at the last minute to resolve the problem of the book" (1990, 18). Similarly, Deborah E. McDowell (1986) finds the resolution of the plot to be stereotyped and unauthentic.

As Angelou admits, her view of Africa is not completely authentic. At times she romanticizes her experiences: "But whether I like it or not, I am also captured by the romance of history" ("Icon" 1997). In *Even the Stars Look Lonesome*, she describes the illusion called Africa: "Despite a spate of nature commentaries, and despite endless shelves of travel books, Africa remains for most of us a hazy and remote illusion" (65).

In Ghana, Angelou was to some degree, and quite reasonably so, caught up in a vision of Africa similar to what a generation of black Americans experienced at home in the 1960s: identification with the Pan-African Movement and with West African hair styles, clothing, language, music, and other manifestations of African culture. In *Traveling Shoes* she embraced these styles, hair and dress in particular. In one revealing ep-isode, Angelou is at first horrified when her beautician, Comfort Adday, styles her hair into ugly strands like the "pickaninnies" in old photos (37). Comfort, apparently amused, goes on to reshape, tighten, and cut Angelou's hair so that by the end of the session her customer looks just like a Ghanaian. Angelou self-consciously recalls this moment, knowing that to "look like" a Ghanaian meant only a cosmetic transformation and not a genuine assimilation into West African attitudes and traditions. It seems that here and in other episodes of *Traveling Shoes*, the contradic-tions of race, culture, and nationality are too strong to disappear and too fragile to preserve.

The ambivalent conclusion of *Traveling Shoes* involves her departure not only from Ghana but from Guy as well. Her journey in Africa over, she waits at the Accra airport for the plane to return her to America.

Using the phrase "second leave-taking" (209), she suggests that her awaited voyage from Africa to America is an ironic echo of the voyage long ago, when West African slaves were chained and wrenched from their homeland and families. She parallels her departure from Africa with her departure from Guy, the emotional center of her autobiographies, the son who in *Singin' and Swingin' and Gettin' Merry Like Christmas* she left in America with his grandmother so that she could tour Europe with *Porgy and Bess*. In *Traveling Shoes*, though, she leaves Guy in Africa as she prepares to return to America.

The reversals at the end of *Traveling Shoes* suggest the apparent end of Angelou's mother/son plot. Guy stands apart from her, surrounded by his African friends. In this, her last depiction of Guy in the narratives, Angelou roots him in the culture of Ghana, thus returning him to the place of his ancestors. He is magically transformed from uncooperative son to newly born American African, free to continue his education at the University of Ghana while she is free to explore her potential as performer, poet, spokesperson, and autobiographer.

In a metaphor that effectively captures the mother/son confrontation in this last volume, Angelou compares her maternal role to an apron string, untied and in shreds. The same metaphor might apply to the plot design that ends the autobiography: She waits until the final pages to tie the unstrung narrative threads together, offering her readers a vision of Guy as a lord, perhaps a chief. Angelou seems to create, in this departure scene, a sunny, almost regal atmosphere, as if to protect herself from acknowledging the reality of so absolute a separation. In giving her son back to Africa, to his ancestors, she appears to be constructing a perfect ending. Instead, it seems to fall short of the forthright self-assessment that readers have come to expect in her autobiographies. As in her dissolving romance with Africa, her farewell address to Guy shows the rough ends of the narrative are still unravelled.

As Maya Angelou brings the mother/son confrontation to its paradoxical conclusion, readers observe that it is the mother who finally does forsake the son, in order to rediscover the special rhythms of her African American heritage. While some critics praise Angelou for her show of independence, others question the willful cutting of the maternal ties that she established throughout the series. When asked about this paradox, Angelou emphatically stated that "If you are really a mother you can let go. It's like love of any sort" ("Icon" 1997).

At the threshold of the New World, Maya Angelou readies herself for departure, letting readers go now that the conflicting elements of point of view and narrative structure have been settled. Ironically, though, the book ends not in departure but in stasis. Without her son, and without full acknowledgment of her Ghanaian heritage, she stands at the edge of Africa, at the Accra airport, with the journey westward anticipated but not accomplished, with the narrative actually unfinished.

What Angelou the autobiographer does not recount is yet another story. It involves the plane that in actuality arrived, at the Accra airport. The Pan Am plane had come via Johannesburg, South Africa. There were Boers [white Dutch South Africans] on the plane:

> They tried their best to keep the blacks sitting together and not intruding on the flight. . . . I had been away from that idea of prejudice and segregation for years. I had been in Egypt and in Ghana and getting on that plane, leaving my son and all, and finding myself in the atmosphere of Arkansas. ("Icon" 1997)

The joys of departure surrender to the horrors of reentry—of much more to come. Despite the feel of an ending, the structure of *All God's Children Need Traveling Shoes* is open to a continuation of the plot into a conceivable sixth volume.

CHARACTER DEVELOPMENT

Angelou's intense suffering over Guy's injury sets both the tone for this pensive fifth volume and greatly reinforces the strength of her character. She first describes herself negatively, in terms of darkness and shadows. She is a "dark spectre" who walks the sweltering white streets (4). A shadow, a ghost, Angelou is reduced to silence. Readers need to interpret the silence not only as a present response but also as a duplication of the past. For her silence is reminiscent of her muteness following the rape by Mr. Freeman described in *I Know Why the Caged Bird Sings*, and of her unspoken terror in *The Heart of a Woman* when friend and novelist John Killens telephones Maya in Chicago to warn her of a crisis between Guy and a Brooklyn gang.

Angelou develops her self-portrait through a combination of present incidents and past recollections, in which events and responses are often meant to recall earlier moments. Thus, in *Traveling Shoes* she thinks warmly of her mother, Vivian Baxter, remembering how she had instructed her Maya and Bailey in the art of survival, much as Maya has instructed Guy, and how Vivian was her "doting mother" (151). On her journey through rural East Ghana she remembers the compassion her grandmother, Annie Henderson, had shown to African Americans traveling during segregation, when they were denied bed, board, food, and decent toilets. When Maya and her roommates reluctantly hire a village boy named Kojo to do housework, she associates his intense color and delicate hands with her brother Bailey.

Kojo is also an obvious substitute for Guy, previously her in-house son, now grown and at university, out of his mother's reach. Maya comments on her feelings for Kojo: "[T]he old became new and I was pinched back into those familiar contractions" (57). In this passage she uses birth images—"pinched" and "contractions"—to describe the painful effect of Kojo's presence and of Guy's past on her own rebirth.

Sometimes the reference to a family member is barely perceptible, as in her recollection that African Americans who appear childlike might actually be acting bravely, like "humming a jazz tune while walking into a gathering of the Ku Klux Klan" (76). The tactic of humming as a way to dissipate fear is an unmistakable analogy to the scene in *I Know Why the Caged Bird Sings* where Mama outlasts the three "powhitetrash" children by humming a hymn (23–27). Or, Angelou laughs at the idea of her father, Bailey Johnson Sr., leaving the comfort of San Diego to make the acquaintance of her suitor, Sheikhali, as required by Malian custom. She remembers that Bailey Sr. believed Africa was inhabited by "savages" (94).

As in the four previous autobiographies, Maya's character in *Traveling Shoes* is tested and determined through her actual and remembered confrontations with her son Guy. She seems to vacillate between wanting to supervise him and wanting to let him go. When she learns, for instance, that Guy is having an affair with a woman a year older than herself, she is so angry that she threatens to strike him. Guy simply patronizes her, calling her his "little mother" and politely insisting on his autonomy (*Traveling Shoes* 149).

In another painful moment from the same book, Guy cooks Maya a fried chicken dinner on her return from Germany and then announces that he has made plans for the evening. Again she is "speechless," unable to respond to Guy's words (186). Alone and unhappy, as she was at the conclusion of *The Heart of a Woman*, Angelou analyzes her feelings toward her son and questions the strength of their love for each other. So adept at expressing her sorrow over Guy's accident, she again verbalizes her pain, although in this case not in dread of her son's impending death but of his growing up, stretching beyond her ability to love or control him. This fluctuation is apparent earlier, in *Singin' and Swingin' and Gettin' Merry Like Christmas*, where Angelou eloquently captures the feelings of guilt that a working mother experiences in slighting her child. Antithetically, in this fifth volume, she conveys her fear that it is the mother who will be slighted.

It is largely this ability to connect emotionally, as mother and woman, that makes Maya Angelou so popular an autobiographer. She has the ability to communicate her misfortunes and make them accessible to sensitive readers, whatever their race or gender. She has the verbal power, through her own self-portrait of a black woman, to eradicate many of the surrounding stereotypes by "demonstrating the trials, rejections, and endurances which so many Black women share" (O'Neale 1984, 26).

Through much of the fifth volume, Angelou's time-consuming concern for her son is paralleled by her efforts to form new relationships with black women. In Ghana she shares a bungalow with two roommates, Vicki Garvin and Alice Windom. Both Alice and Vicki were educated in America; Alice having a master's degree from the University of Chicago and Vicki a master's in economics along with a national reputation in labor organizing. Yet neither woman is able to get the kind of work in Ghana that reflects their capabilities. Angelou considers herself lucky to have been hired by the University of Ghana as an administrative assistant and lecturer. Although the job does not include tuition or other privileges, she confesses that she loves getting paid just to look at the currency, with its portrait of a black president.

Fortunately, Angelou is able to find an American enclave in Ghana where she can express her shifting impressions of the country and of her place in it. Humorously dubbed the Revolutionist Returnees, the small group of African American expatriates recognizes her struggles—the conflicting feelings of being "home" yet simultaneously being "homeless," cut off from America without tangible roots in their adopted black nation. Of her various friendships with the African Americans, she is closest to author and journalist Julian Mayfield. Like Angelou, Mayfield and his wife, Ana Livia, are identified with a movement that would enable future African Americans to live again on African soil. Sadly, Mayfield did not "come home" to Africa. He died in the United States in 1984, where he had accepted a position at Howard University, an historically black institution located in Washington, D.C., an ocean away from the promised land.

Angelou was also a friend of the revered American writer, W.E.B. Du Bois. Du Bois was one of the twentieth century's most influential theorists of black thought and philosophy. Author, critic, editor, Du Bois was best known for his book *The Souls of Black Folk* (1903), in which he described an American Negro culture rich in mythology, music, and spiritual traditions. He also was instrumental in promoting African American writers and artists during the Harlem Renaissance (1919 to 1929), in his role as editor of the journal, *The Crisis*. Unlike the Mayfields and many other expatriates, Du Bois and his wife, Shirley Graham, found sanctuary in Africa when, shortly after Ghana claimed independence in 1957, President Kwame Nkrumah (1909–1972) offered them permanent residency. "To many of us," exclaims Angelou, "he was the first American Negro intellectual" (124). An advocate of world peace, Du Bois joined the Communist Party in the early 1960s. With Du Bois as an accessible model, Angelou rekindles her own leadership qualities, which were at their height when she had been Northern Coordinator of Martin Luther King's Southern Christian Leadership Conference, but which had understandably diminished following her commitment to Vus Make and her anguish over Guy's accident.

Angelou seems resentful of Du Bois's wife, comparing her to Africa's tallest mountain, Kilimanjaro, a comparison she also used in describing Vusumzi Make's patronizing attitude toward her; Vus was "the Old Man of Kilimanjaro" and Maya a tiny shepherd (McPherson 1990, 98). The highest mountain in Africa—majestic, remote, located in Tanzania—Kilimanjaro appears to be an appropriate symbol for Maya's distaste of Shirley Graham's isolationist profile. Maya's hostility will create problems for Angelou later in *Traveling Shoes*.

Although geographically far from America and disillusioned by Dr. King's nonviolent strategies, Angelou nonetheless makes a commitment to his 1963 march on Washington. In a show of support for his internationally publicized civil-rights demonstration, she and a small group of African American friends—Julian Mayfield, Alice Windom, Ana Livia, and others—organize a parallel demonstration in Ghana. Noticeably shifting her perspective from "I" to "we," Angelou outlines their plans, which include writing a letter of protest against racism and conveying it to the American ambassador. Sadly, their enthusiasm for King's historic project is dampened by their denunciation of his pacifist tactics; they hated their experiences in America of being harassed by whites, then being told to be passive about it. As Angelou told Marney Rich, King's idea of "redemptive suffering" seemed irresponsible; she had never seen a person redeemed through anguish (1989, 127). Despite her own restrained participation in the protest, Angelou renews her tenuous bonds with King, a commitment that helps prepare her psychologically for her later allegiance to Malcolm X, so vividly described a few pages later in the text.

For the African Americans in Ghana, Dr. King's march has grievous emotional repercussions. On the night before the Ghanaian Solidarity Demonstration, as King is about to achieve his greatest public triumph, W.E.B. Du Bois, weak, ailing, and five years shy of one hundred years of age, dies. When they learn of his death, the Revolutionist Returnees transform a politically restrained rally into a wake to commemorate the spirit of a man who made immeasurable contributions to African American life and letters. One participant starts to sing "Oh, oh, Freedom" and is joined by the diverse crowd, which includes farmers, vacationers, teachers, students, even Guy, who has had training in protest marches. Angelou writes about this ceremony using the collective form: "We were singing Dr. Du Bois' spirit, for the invaluable contributions he made, for his shining intellect and his courage" (124). This great American editor and statesman had become a symbol to African Americans living in Ghana, for he had been welcomed to the promised land, in life and in death.

The tone of the march suddenly shifts, however, from a tribute to Du Bois to an unfounded sunrise tirade against two soldiers, one of them black, who are raising the flag at the American Embassy. The sequence concludes with Angelou's invective against the government of the United States for its centuries of exploitation of black people. At the same time that she chastises the United States, she still longs for full citizenship, which she cannot expect to acquire in Africa. Angelou's alliance with the African American community often focuses on their indignation over the Ghanaians' refusal to fully welcome them.

Angelou and her small group of African American colleagues are the people most involved in the planning for Malcolm X's visit to Ghana in 1964. They help arrange his itinerary and they introduce him to African leaders. When Angelou first met Malcolm X, he had espoused the teachings of Muslim leader Elijah Muhammad, the prophet who claimed that white people were devils. In *The Heart of a Woman*, she vividly depicts Malcolm's initial impact on her: "I had never been so affected by a human presence" (167). In 1964, en route from a pilgrimage to the holy Islamic cities of Mecca and Jiddah, the Black Muslim leader experienced a political transformation. Although he still believed that America is a racist country, he no longer held the conviction that whites were inherently evil.

For Malcolm X, the return visit from Mecca to Cairo to Ghana is intended to garner support from black world leaders for his Organization of African Unity, a nationalist group not directly governed by the Nation of Islam. He also wishes to contest racist tactics within the diaspora—those areas occupied by displaced peoples of African descent. In a complicated sequence in *All God's Children Need Traveling Shoes*, Angelou cites several references to the slave trade from Malcolm X's speeches in Ghana. If racism in America ceased, he argued, then the civil-rights movement would be as unnecessary as the public sale of slaves once was. Malcolm X stressed the unity of all black people, encouraging Angelou to come home and organize his political alliance, as she had once coordinated Martin Luther King's.

His congenial manner dwindles, though, when Angelou, as she drives him to the airport, makes some injudicious remarks about middle-class black organizations like the Urban League and the NAACP. He further admonishes her criticism of Shirley Graham, Du Bois's still mourning widow, for failing to relate to the African American protest movement. Once again Angelou expressed bitterness at Shirley Graham's prestige among the Ghanaians, having earlier compared her to Kilimanjaro. Malcolm X bluntly labels her comments "very childish, dangerously immature" (144). Stung by his scolding, she is in tears. After his departure from Ghana, she avoids any personal analysis of Malcolm X's chastisement, using the collective rather than the singular pronoun to describe the sadly altered state of the so-called Revolutionist Returnees. Malcolm's parting reduced them to "a little group of Black folks, looking for a home" (146).

Angelou draws on vivid episodes like the visit of Malcolm X to create dynamic characters. These confrontations, interspersed within her own larger narrative of self-development, read like short stories or vignettes. Most of them are focused not on renowned world leaders but on the natives of Accra and its outskirts.

Angelou's interchange with the African houseboy, Kojo, is the most delightful of these character sketches, since it entangles her once again in a reluctant maternal role. She is required to go to Kojo's school to discuss his grades with the headmaster. She, Vicki, and Alice are coaxed into supervising homework assignments in math and mapmaking. Maya is forced into a dialogue with a mere boy of fourteen, who insists on his right to debate personal issues such as whether she should or should not accept the gift of a refrigerator from her Malian suitor.

For two months Angelou assumes that the often irritating houseboy is poor and that he is manipulating her. To her surprise, in the yard one morning she discovers a group of richly clad people who are Kojo's relatives, who have come with container upon container of vegetables to thank Maya and her roommates for helping educate him. "Auntie Maya" is so struck by the splendor of the gifting ceremony that she falls apart after the family leaves. She lies in bed drinking gin and pitying the unwanted children of Africa.

Angelou's relationships with contemporary Africans have a positive effect on her self-awareness and her personal growth. Seeing Maya's disintegration following Guy's car crash, Julian Mayfield reproaches her for becoming a wreck: "Hell, it's Guy whose neck is broken. Not yours" (10). He introduces her to a prominent African woman, folklorist Efua Sutherland, director of the National Theater of Ghana, a woman of compassion and sensitivity. Their friendship is spontaneous from the start. Through the solace of Brother Mayfield and Sister Sutherland, Maya is able to cry for the first time since Guy's accident. Sutherland retains a strong connection throughout the autobiography, offering advice and reinforcing Angelou's sense of belonging to the Ghanaian intellectual community. Angelou strengthens their friendship by helping design costumes and train actors at Efua's National Theatre.

A less typical friendship involves Comfort Adday, neither a colleague nor an intellectual but a stenographer/hairdresser. Comfort is lively and amusing; she loves to laugh and tease Maya about her age, her hair, her single child, and her sex life. Regrettably, Comfort starts to lose weight and strength over a period of several months. She confesses to Maya that she is the victim of a spell put on her by her lover's wife and leaves for Sierra Leone to consult a woman who will cleanse her and remove the voodoo spell. Refusing Angelou's offer of money, she requests only that her client be there when she returns. A few weeks later Maya learns that Comfort died in Sierra Leone.

Another short-lived friendship is with Grace Nuamah. Ghana's most esteemed folk dancer, Nuamah has the responsibility of performing at major state functions. She also teaches dance at the Institute of African Studies at the University of Ghana, where Angelou holds her job of administrative assistant. One day Nuamah announces that her faculty pay is missing. Maya later recovers Grace's missing money, which she discovers in a brown envelope on the desk. In thanks, Nuamah generously introduces Maya to a Mr. Abatanu.

Unfortunately, Abatanu dislikes Maya's directness and she his pretensions. After the failed matchmaking, Grace expresses disappointment with Maya's behavior, for she had offered the valuable male friend as a favor. A woman trained in African traditions, insists Grace, would have accepted the kind offer. Angelou's insensitivity to African customs signals the end of their closeness. She mentions Grace Nuamah only one more time in the text, listing her among the group of colleagues bidding her farewell at the Accra airport.

Angelou is not always so discouraging when approached by African men. Recalling her affectionate portrayals of dancing partner R. L. Poole in *Gather Together in My Name* and of fiancé Thomas Allen and Allen's rival Vus Make, in *The Heart of a Woman*, it is apparent that she has enjoyed her physical intimacy with black men. The most romantically depicted male in *Traveling Shoes* is Sheikhali, a wealthy importer from Mali, a country southwest of Ghana. She describes him as "sublimely handsome," very tall, with dark skin and elegant robes (66). She agrees to go to his apartment and soon afterward Sheikhali proposes marriage, but there is a hitch. As is customary among Muslim men in West Africa, he already has eight children from two women, only one of them his wife. He wants Maya to be his second wife, willing to adapt to the marriage customs of Mali and reject her "White woman way" of being impatient (94). As a strong and independent woman, Maya finds his proposition unacceptable.

Many of the African men whom she admires are prominent in Ghanaian politics. She is an ardent supporter of Kwame Nkrumah, the Ghanaian president who helped found the Pan-African Movement in the 1940s and 1950s and the Organization of African Unity in 1963. His leadership was overthrown in 1966, a few years after Angelou's departure. After he was deposed, Angelou stated that her presence there would be unstablizing and that she would not return (Caruana 1989, 33).

The legendary Nana Nketsia satisfies Angelou's yearning for a place within both cultures. He holds impressive British degrees and is the first African vice chancellor of the University of Ghana; at the same time he is a tribal leader, paramount chief of the Ahanta people of Ghana. One evening Nana Nketsia sends his chauffeur to Maya's bungalow with instructions that she come to his *Ahenfie*, the "house of the Nana" (108). She is impressed with the elegant sofas and spacious surroundings. He introduces her to nationally recognized poet Kwesi Brew. During the conversation, Nana reveals his booming voice and his fierce pride at being an African, what Angelou ironically calls "the passion of self-appreciation" (110). Kwesi Brew, more even tempered, explains Ghanaian traditions and proposes a toast in honor of the African character. These two powerful men appear occasionally in the book. Brew, in fact, becomes a special friend, someone who protects her when they travel together. Angelou repeated to an interviewer what Brew said about her to a foreign authority: "She may not be a Ghanaian, but she is a sister" (Randall-Tsuruta 1989, 106). Both Nana and Brew participate in her send-off at the Accra airport.

Most of Angelou's encounters with African women and men are positive ones that contribute to her growing intoxication with Africa as she tries to learn about her heritage. Angelou's identification with the Mother Continent is personal and patriotic. Her stature and skin color, indicate her African ancestry, but so do the cultural contributions of American/African people, whose blues songs, shouts, and gospels echo the rhythms of West Africa. Le Roi Jones affirmed the connection between African and American Negro music in his book *Blues People* (1963), when he wrote that the blues and other black forms "could not exist if the African captives had not become American captives" (17).

Maya Angelou, as both narrator and central character in her own story, is concerned with capturing the rhythms of Africa as they affect her reinvigorated ties with her ancestors. In her travels through West Africa she discovers certain connections between her American traditions and those of her ancestors. She considers herself almost home when an African woman, Foriwa, identifies her as one of the Bambara group on the basis of similarities in height, hair, and skin color. She connects with a number of African mother figures, among them Patience Aduah, who, like Momma Henderson, is generous in giving away food to the people of her village.

When she first comes to Accra Angelou wants to nestle into Ghana "as a baby nuzzles in a mother's arms" (19). This fantasy subsides as she realizes that the Ghanaians are not interested in extending the embrace. She notices that the black Americans in her group share similar delusions of being loved by the Ghanaians. The Revolutionist Returnees come to Africa full of desire, and hate being ignored or misunderstood in their new home.

Always in search of home, Angelou realizes that she must remain a while longer in Ghana if she is to uncover the fullness of spirit and depth of character toward which she strives. Her ambivalent attitude toward living in Ghana provides *Traveling Shoes* with its richness of texture and depth of analysis. Angelou invariably tries to make connections to decrease the differences between the culture of the ancestors and the culture of the slaves.

When Angelou listens to one of Nana Nketsia's speeches, for instance, she notices that the chief's majestic voice captures the rhythms of black preachers and that the African experience is similar to her own background. She is caught between identifying with things African and using African culture as a way to acknowledge the abandoned country of her birth. Her need, here and elsewhere, to underline Ghanaian associations with African American parallels demonstrates what Dolly A. McPherson calls Maya's "double-consciousness"—a vision of her self containing both African and American components (1990, 113). Through her identification with Africa, Angelou finds the context in which to explore her selfhood and to reaffirm the meaning of motherhood.

Angelou's self-discovery is augmented when she temporarily leaves the African continent in the mid 1960s to tour Berlin and Venice in a limited number of performances of Genet's *The Blacks* with the original cast. Her view of Berlin involves a meticulously drawn account of the German mentality, which is balanced against the warm reunion with the original off-Broadway cast, among them familiar names such as Cicely Tyson, the star of *Sounder* (1972) and the *Autobiography of Miss Jane Pittman* (1974); Lou Gossett Jr., who has had numerous supporting or leading film roles, including *The Deep* (1977) and *An Officer and a Gentleman* (1982); and the actor James Earl Jones, more recognized today as the voice of Darth Vadar in the *Star Wars* series (1977–1983) and for his throaty commercials for Bell Atlantic than for his outstanding performances in such films as *The Great White Hope* (1970) and *Matewan* (1987).

In the foreign, theatrical setting of Berlin, Angelou revives her passion for African American culture and values, putting them into perspective as she weighs them against Germany's history of military aggression. In 1914, in the First World War, Germany, in alliance with Austria-Hungary and several other nations, declared war on France and Russia. Twenty-five years later, in 1939, Germany occupied Czechoslovakia and then Poland. In the Second World War, more than six million Jews were exterminated because the leader of the Nazi party, Adolf Hitler (1889–1945), deemed Jews, as well as Negroes and Gypsies as racially inferior.

Angelou and the other actors angrily recalled the story of U.S. athlete Jesse Owens, the track star who won four gold medals in the Olympic games of 1936, which were held in Berlin. Owens set several Olympic

records during these games, as well as a world record with the United
States 400-meter relay team. But Hitler, then chancellor of Germany, refused to recognize Owens's triumphs because they invalidated his theory
of a master race—a race of Aryans genetically superior to other ethnic
groups. On the argument that Jesse Owens was racially inferior, Hitler
denied the athlete his rightful claim to the medals.

One morning, fortified by the presence of an uninvited Israeli actor
named Torvash, Maya accepts a breakfast invitation with a well-to-do
German family whom she suspects shares similar notions of racial inferi-
ority. At the gathering, family members and guests take turns telling stories about race. Angelou relates the Brer Rabbit story in which the
threatened animal outwits the oppressor. The German tells a parable in
which a bird, symbolizing a Jew, is trampled in dung. The verbal violence
of the narratives escalates to such a point that Angelou becomes sick in the
garden. Her disgust is by no means lessened when she learns that the host,
a collector of African art, has only invited her to his home because he
hopes that she will get him some good buys in Ghanaian folk art.

Angelou says little about the performances in Venice, other than to
mention the disturbing fact that angry protesters picketed *The Blacks* for
its sexual content, calling Genet's play "filth" (175). Despite the potential
for confrontation, the cast manages to go onstage without major incident.
The theater sequence ends and Angelou retraces her steps, reentering
Africa by way of Egypt. Although her character growth is primarily nurtured in a West African setting, her encounters in Italy and especially in
Germany help shape and broaden her constantly changing vision. The
mixture of fascist surroundings, black performances, and Jewish survival
sharpens her perceptions of African Americans at home and abroad.
These perceptions contribute to her reclaiming herself and her evolution
as a citizen of the world. The universality of experience in *Traveling Shoes*
anticipates, to some degree, the acclaimed poem, "On the Pulse of Morning," read three decades later at the 1993 inauguration of President Bill
Clinton. In this powerful ode, Angelou addresses all the people of the
world, including the Germans. The evocative poem has a worldly wise
maturity to it, a wisdom that must be attributed in part to her knowledge
of the countless places she has been.

As a character, Maya clearly demonstrates her maturity in *Traveling
Shoes*. She matures as a mother who, concerned for the well-being of her
son, is apparently willing to let him go his own way, both in terms of
his sexual options and his determination to reside in Ghana. She matures
as a woman, no longer the victim of good-looking men but one who can

assess mutual motives and feelings. She matures as an American, able to perceive the roots of her identity and capable of cultivating those roots into a consciousness that affects her whole personality.

THEMATIC ISSUES

The themes that Angelou develops most fully in her fifth volume are motherhood, race, and the search for an African identity. As we have seen throughout this work, motherhood is Angelou's most consistent theme and in *Traveling Shoes* it is consistently presented, from its beginning where Maya awaits reports of her son's injuries, to its close, where she ends her conflict with her son, bidding him farewell. The theme of motherhood does not, however, consume the text, as it does in *Gather Together in My Name* or *Singin' and Swingin' and Gettin' Merry Like Christmas*.

In *Traveling Shoes*, perhaps because she is a seasoned mother or perhaps because she is looking for a positive way to close the series, Angelou develops a theme of motherhood which suggests liberation. Her initial response to Guy's announced independence is to retreat quietly into the corners of his life, knowing that she can no longer keep him under her wing. These feelings are complicated by a mutual recognition that part of motherhood is letting go: they both need to be free of one another. The narrator keeps confrontation at a minimum, with the mother/child opposition dramatized only twice, first, when she challenges Guy with the news that he is having an affair, and second, when he announces, following her return from the Genet tour, that Maya's mothering is finished and that his life "belongs to me" (186).

It seems that by the time the autobiography ends, Guy has reached that stage of development where, as one of God's children, he has earned the right to wear traveling shoes. While these shoes will carry him away from his mother, they simultaneously confirm his autonomy, his independence. Yet it is not the end, for as Angelou insists, motherhood is never over. From her account of Guy's car accident, to her affectionate remarks about her own mother and grandmother, to placing her son in an Africa from which she herself felt excluded, Angelou infuses her autobiographies with maternal consciousness. What is more, the theme of motherhood is reflected in numerous subthemes: Angelou's affection for Kojo, the Ghanaian houseboy; her delight in being called by the African title "Auntie" by Nana Nketsia's charming children and other children from Cairo or the outskirts of Accra. The phrase has a maternal connotation that pleases her.

In *Traveling Shoes*, the theme of motherhood parallels the theme of race, indicated on one level by Angelou's quest for acceptance by Mother Africa. The paradoxical term Mother Africa, which she uses occasionally, is a popular one that has been articulated by numerous West African and American writers of this century. The Senegalese poet David Diop, for example, uses the phrase as both title and subject in "Africa (to my Mother)" (1961). From a more critical perspective, race is a theme through which Angelou illustrates connections and confrontations. She extends her awareness of racial antagonisms to include not only the struggles between Africans and Americans but also between Germans and Jews. The racial components of these cultures, interwoven and inseparable, provide Angelou with rich opportunities for thematic development.

Finally, Angelou links racial matters to her relationship with Africa and to her desire to be rooted. The Dark Continent calls so loudly that it becomes a desired presence, embodied in the figures of a dancer, a chief, a laughing ancestor. Lyman B. Hagen, in his 1997 book on Angelou, compares her quest for identity to the one Alex Haley describes in *Roots* (1976), a book that heavily influenced African American attitudes toward Africa. However, becoming African is an unattainable goal that falls outside of her desire for assimilation: "Whether she likes it or not, she begins to discover that she is a Black American, and that in Africa she is a Black American in exile" (McPherson 1990, 113).

Woven into her self-discovery are her feelings of guilt as a citizen of the United States of America, a country instrumental in maintaining a slave trade for almost 250 years. By extension, the theme of racial identity encompasses a variety of other motifs: ancestry, cultural differences, suffering, inequality, and homecoming. These thematic issues function simultaneously with plot to lend a dynamic configuration to Angelou's autobiographical statements.

STYLE AND LITERARY DEVICES

In *Traveling Shoes* Angelou makes superb use of language in recording moments of emotional intensity. At the beginning of the narrative she describes going back and forth from the hospital, emerging from the cool interior into the bright sunlight as she herself drifts in and out of her son's pain, which is also her pain. During the summer of 1962 she feels "gobbled" down. The days remind her of "fat men yawning after a sumptuous dinner" (4).

Later, she records the horrors of slavery as she travels through western Ghana, known for Cape Coast Castle and Elmina Castle, former holding forts for slaves. Angelou imaginatively captures the agony of being a slave. She observes the now quiet forts and envisions bloodied people, silently enduring their chains: "They lived in a mute territory, dead to feeling and protest" (97). The potency of the passage is reinforced through simple language and repeated images of silence, an image Angelou has used in other volumes. Her use of the word mute emphasizes the silent misery of the slaves and Angelou's connection to them and their agony. Her written words in this eulogy attempt to break the silence of that "mute territory" inhabited by the enslaved Africans, who were never free to respond to their assailants or to narrate the grim story of their captivity.

Angelou's language in capturing the final separation from Africa of her ancestors has an awesome potency, a feeling of loss. But she does not allow the book to end on a desolate note, choosing instead to create, in the last full paragraph, a praise song that stands apart from her softer, more subtle style. In an extremely condensed history of slavery in America, she evokes the blues, the dance, the gospel, as they were carried through the streets of Massachusetts and Alabama, changed but still African; for Africa is still in the body and in the hips, in a "wide open laughter" (209). This passage, which represents the author at her most jubilant, is followed by one simple concluding statement: "I could nearly hear the old ones chuckling" (209). In a book that constantly alternates between African and African American voices, Angelou gives the last words to the "old ones," to her Ghanaian ancestors, but filtered through her own experiences and the rich traditions of the spiritual and cultural forms that are part of the oral folk tradition. Yet her identification with the oral tradition of West Africa is not a permanent choice. For Angelou recognizes, at the end of *All God's Children Need Traveling Shoes*, that if she is to become a contemporary writer, she must put on her traveling shoes for the long journey home.

ALTERNATIVE READING: SIGNIFYING AND THE
BLACK TRADITION

In 1984 the influential critic Henry Louis Gates Jr. published an essay, "The Blackness of Blackness: A Critique of the Sign of the Signifying

Monkey." This essay, which became the foundation for Gates's 1988 book, *The Signifying Monkey: A Theory of African-American Literary Criticism*, is a crucial text in the development of black literary criticism. His essay helped transform black studies into a sophisticated procedure for examining and categorizing African American literature.

Gates applies the term signifying or "signifyin(g)," to the functions of black speech patterns as well as the process of echoing earlier African American traditions, motifs, or figures of speech within a particular text. The trickster, the Signifying Monkey, is a descendent of Esu-Elegbara, the West African figure who "dwells at the margins of discourse, ever punning, ever troping, ever embodying the ambiguities of language" (1984, 286). Signifying is a message system, a strategy of communication. As its emissary, the Signifying Monkey is the conveyer of multiple meanings and interpretations in the literature of the African diaspora—areas populated by black Africans as a result of the slave trade.

Angelou, who is familiar with the term signifying, uses it to describe the way in which older black women—much like Gates's African-born trickster monkey—use words and speech patterns to assert their verbal power: "The process is called signifying, and has an African origin" (*Stars* 137–38). One might attribute Angelou's abundant verbal punning in the autobiographies to her signifying self: to her verbal power as she portrays the power and duality of her relationships.

Gates's sensitivity to signifying in African American literature allows him to unveil the repeated black verbal patterns in Zora Neale Hurston's *Their Eyes Were Watching God* (1937), a book whose forerunners, he claims, are Frederick Douglass's *Narrative of the Life of Frederick Douglass* (1845) and W.E.B. Du Bois's novel, *The Quest of the Silver Fleece* (1911). Gates, who convincingly demonstrates the signifying connection between Alice Walker's *The Color Purple* (1982) and Hurston's *Their Eyes Were Watching God* (1937), believes that critics of African American literature must read modern texts against earlier African American ones. He argues that "Our literary tradition exists, because of these precisely chartable formal literary relationships, relationships of signifying" (1984, 290).

In the search for illustrations of signifying in the African American literary tradition, the slave narrative is a particularly fertile source. Although Gates does not refer to Maya Angelou in either "The Blackness of Blackness" or *The Signifying Monkey*, other critics discuss her echoing of the slave narrative. Dolly A. McPherson, for example, argues that the similarities between Angelou's autobiographies and slave narratives result from their sharing "a quest that will encourage the development of an authentic self" (1990, 121). Selwyn R. Cudjoe stresses this connection by citing a quote from a slave narrative to introduce his 1984 essay on Angelou and autobiography. It is also relevant that Angelou confirmed these opinions when she told interviewer George Plimpton (1990; rpt. 1994) that she was "following a tradition established by Frederick Douglass—the slave narrative" (16).

Chapter 2 discusses Angelou's use of this form in relationship to slave narratives by Olaudah Equiano, Frederick Douglass, and Harriet Jacobs, whose pen name was Linda Brent. This alternative reading focuses on Brent's *Incidents in the Life of a Slave Girl* (1861), in an attempt to illustrate the process of signifying, a critical method that uncovers and analyzes earlier black literary patterns in contemporary texts.

In *All God's Children Need Traveling Shoes*, Angelou reiterates certain familiar patterns of the African American slave narrative—the journey; the quest for freedom; empathy for the horrors suffered by slaves. Angelou's outrage against slavery, expressed in the Cape Coast Castle passage and elsewhere, repeats the condemnation of the slave system recorded by articulate slave narrators in the eighteenth and nineteenth centuries in America. The condemnation of slavery is central to Brent's plot. In her chapter on local slaveholders she describes the kinds of punishment to which slaves were submitted: They were burned by being hung in the air over a fire; clubbed or starved or mauled to death; tied to a tree in the freezing wind. A woman slave had no value other than to reproduce. If she refused she was whipped or shot. Women, reports Brent, "are on a par with animals" (1861, 380).

Brent's focus, like Angelou's a century later, is on motherhood—on the need to preserve one's offspring. Despite escaping, Brent is unable to desert her children. For seven years in her journey to freedom Linda Brent is immobile, concealed in a windowless garret, unable to touch the children who play below her gaze. Brent's greatest source of anguish, greater than the threat of being raped and beaten by her master, Dr. Flint, is her fear of losing her children.

The slave mother's misery throughout the garret narrative is mental and physical. Mentally, she doubts that she will be reunited with her family; physically, her cramped body, pinned in the attic and exposed to wind and rain, duplicates her constricted mental state—as it duplicates the anguish of any African bound by the shackles of the slave system. In a section titled "The Children Sold" Brent depicts the torment of separation: "I bit my lips till the blood came to keep from crying out.

Were my children with their grandmother, or had the speculator carried them off? The suspense was dreadful" (111). She compares this moment to "the darkest cloud that hung over my life" (112).

In *All God's Children Need Traveling Shoes*, Maya Angelou, like Linda Brent before her, occupies a restricted geographical space. Confined to Ghana because of Guy's car accident, her solitary visits to his hospital room echo Brent's lonely contemplation over the loss of her daughter, Ellen, sold as a child to another master. Admittedly, Angelou is more privileged than the slave women who endured the atrocities of the plantation system. But her roots in that system, rediscovered during her journey through eastern Ghana, are vivid reminders of being descended from slavery.

Other critics have touched on the similarities and differences between Harriet Jacobs/Linda Brent and Maya Angelou, particularly in the related themes of rape, separation, confinement, and black womanhood. Mary Vermillion, for example, argues that both autobiographers challenge the racial stereotypes inherent in white literature by celebrating the black female and transforming personal suffering into a symbol for the confinement of African Americans in general (1992, 250).

It is also important, in a discussion of signifying, to mention Angelou's debt to Zora Neale Hurston's *Their Eyes Were Watching God*, a novel filled with dramatic episodes and dominated by the themes of travel, female strength, male/female relationships, and the quest for a home. Like Hurston, Angelou accumulates a vast array of characters, events, and themes in *Traveling Shoes*. In a panoramic sweep, Hurston creates a unique vision of black life in Florida, and Angelou offers especially in her last three autobiographies, a wide-lens view of Africa and central Europe, recorded by an African American woman. At the end of *Their Eyes Were Watching God*, Janie Crawford, the central character, uses the metaphor of the fishnet to illustrate how she must gather together the memories of her world: "She pulled in her horizon like a great fish-net. Pulled it from around the waist of the world and draped it over her shoulder" (184). Maya Angelou, at the edge of the airport in West Africa, on the eastern shore of the Great Atlantic, waits, like her foremother, to drape her memories over her writer's shoulder and bear them home.

In the last several pages of *Traveling Shoes*, Maya Angelou signifies the slave within herself as she narrates her effect on certain Africans, descended from a plundered people, who, having heard her voice, recognized her as a relative. At the same time, she praises the African

American culture born of that history and senses that as an artist and writer, she has a designated place within it, that she signifies it.

Angelou's journey from Africa back to America is in certain ways a restatement of the historical phase known as mid-passage, when slaves were brutally transported in ships from West Africa to the so-called New World. Angelou shows a deep identification with the victims of mid-passage. Remnants of that journey burn in her memory, shaping her identity with her ancestors and the structure of the autobiography itself.

Part of her narrative mission is to take the stories of Africans back with her to the United States, to those whose ancestors survived the horrendous transportation of slaves from West Africa to the Americas. In returning from Accra, as Malcolm X advised, Angelou is able to bring to her country a first-hand account of a continent that most African Americans have deeply felt but rarely visited. Her memorable search for roots reverberates now, as it did then, through her countless interviews on television, in periodicals, and in the popular press. As one of the best known of all contemporary autobiographers, Maya Angelou extends a tradition initiated by slaves and continually reimaged by popular writers of African descent.

Bibliography

WORKS BY MAYA ANGELOU

Autobiographies

All God's Children Need Traveling Shoes. New York: Random, 1986.
Gather Together in My Name. New York: Random, 1974.
The Heart of a Woman. New York: Random, 1981.
I Know Why the Caged Bird Sings. New York: Random, 1970.
Singin' and Swingin' and Gettin' Merry Like Christmas. New York: Random, 1976.

Musings

Even the Stars Look Lonesome. New York: Random, 1997.
Wouldn't Take Nothing for My Journey Now. New York: Random, 1993.

Autobiographical Essays

"My Grandson, Home at Last." *Woman's Day* August 1986: 46–55.
"Why I Moved Back to the South." *Ebony* February 1982: 130–34.

Children's Books

Kofi and His Magic. Photographs by Margaret Courtney-Clarke. New York: Clarkson N. Potter, 1996.

Life Doesn't Frighten Me. With artist Jean-Michel Basquiat. New York: Stewart, 1993.

Mrs. Flowers. With artist Etienne Delessert. Minneapolis, MN: Redpath, 1986.

My Painted House, My Friendly Chicken, and Me. Photographs by Margaret Courtney-Clarke. New York: Clarkson N. Potter, 1994.

Poetry

"A Brave and Startling Truth." Internet. Available: http://w3.arizona.edu/~amun/unpoem.html

And Still I Rise. New York: Random, 1978.

The Complete Collected Poems of Maya Angelou. New York: Random, 1994.

I Shall Not Be Moved. New York: Random, 1990.

Just Give Me a Cool Drink of Water 'Fore I Diiie. New York: Random, 1971.

"Maya Angelou's Million Man March Poem." 16 October 1995. Internet. Available: http://www.lgc.apc.org/africanam/hot/maaya.html

Now Sheba Sings the Song. With artist Tom Feelings. New York: Dutton, 1987.

Oh Pray My Wings Are Gonna Fit Me Well. New York: Random, 1975.

Phenomenal Woman. 1978. New York: Random, 1995.

Poems: Maya Angelou. New York: Random, 1986.

Shaker, Why Don't You Sing? New York: Random, 1983.

Film

Cook, Fielder, dir. *I Know Why the Caged Bird Sings.* Screenplay by Maya Angelou. Learning Corp. America, 1978.

WORKS ABOUT MAYA ANGELOU

Biographical Sources

"Angelou, Maya." *1994 Current Biography Yearbook.* New York: H. W. Wilson, 1994. 25–29.

Bloom, Lynn Z. "Maya Angelou." *Dictionary of Literary Biography.* Vol. 38. Detroit, MI: Gale, 1985. 3–12.

Readings on Maya Angelou. No ed. San Diego, CA: Greenhaven, 1997.

Interviews

Caruana, Stephanie. "Maya Angelou: An Interview." Elliot 29–37.

Chrisman, Robert. "The *Black Scholar* Interviews Maya Angelou." *Black Scholar* 8.4 (January/February 1977): 44–53.

Crane, Tricia. "Maya Angelou." Elliot 173–78.

Crockett, Sandra. "Poetic Angelou Can Sing, Cut a Rug." *Baltimore Sun* 9 Sept. 1997, E1, 8.

Davis, Curt. "Maya Angelou: And Still She Rises." Elliot 68–76.

Elliot, Jeffrey M., ed. *Conversations with Maya Angelou.* Jackson: University Press of Mississippi, 1989.

Forma, Aminatta. "Kicking Ass." Elliot 161–64.

Guy, Rosa. "A Conversation between Rosa Guy and Maya Angelou." Elliot 218–40.

Harris, Russell. "*Zelo* Interviews Maya Angelou." Elliot 165–72.

Kay, Jackie. "The Maya Character." Elliot 194–200.

Kelley, Ken. "Visions: Maya Angelou." *Mother Jones.* http://www.mojones.com/mother_jones/MJ95/kelley.html

Lupton, Mary Jane. "Talking with an Icon: An Interview with Maya Angelou." 16 June 1997. Unpublished.

Moyers, Bill. "Portraits of Greatness." PBS Home Video. Pacific Arts, 1982.

Neubauer, Carol E. "An Interview with Maya Angelou." *Massachusetts Review* 28 (1987): 286–92.

Plimpton, George. "The Art of Fiction CXIX: Maya Angelou." *Paris Review* 32: 116 (1990): 145–67. Rpt. "Maya Angelou with George Plimpton." *Contemporary Literary Criticism* 77 (1994): 14–21.

Randall-Tsuruta, Dorothy. "An Interview with Maya Angelou." Elliot 102–8.

Rich, Marney. "In Maya Angelou, A Caged Bird Sings." Elliot 125–30.

Sarler, Carol. "A Life in the Day of Maya Angelou." Elliot 214–17.

Toppman, Lawrence. "Maya Angelou: The Serene Spirit of a Survivor." Elliot 140–45.

Webster, Valerie. "A Journey Through Life." Elliot 179–82.

Critical Views of the Autobiographies

Chick, Nancy. "Maya Angelou: A Twentieth Century Scheherazade." Master's thesis, University of Georgia, 1992.

Collier, Eugenia. "Maya Angelou: From 'Caged Bird' to 'All God's Children.'" In *New Directions,* a publication of Howard University (October 1986): 22–27.

Hagen, Lyman B. *Heart of a Woman, Mind of a Writer, and Soul of A Poet: A Critical Analysis of the Writings of Maya Angelou.* Lanham, MD: University Press of America, 1997.

Lupton, Mary Jane. "Maya Angelou." In *American Writers Supplement IV, Part 1.* New York: Scribner's, 1996. 1–19.

———. "Singing the Black Mother: Maya Angelou and Autobiographical Continuity." *Black American Literature Forum* 24 (1990): 257–76.

McPherson, Dolly A. *Order Out of Chaos: The Autobiographical Works of Maya Angelou.* New York: Peter Lang, 1990.

Meyers, Linda Mae Zarpentine. "Maya Angelou and the Multiplicity of Self." Master's thesis, Morgan State University, 1995.

O'Neale, Sondra. "Reconstruction of the Composite Self: New Images of Black Women in Maya Angelou's Continuing Autobiography." In *Black Women Writers (1950–1980): A Critical Evaluation*. Ed. Mari Evans. Garden City, NY: Doubleday, 1984. 25–36.

Saunders, James Robert. "Breaking Out of the Cage: The Autobiographical Writings of Maya Angelou." *Hollins Critic* 28:4 (October 1991): 1–10.

Shuker, Nancy. *Maya Angelou*. Englewood Cliffs, NJ: Silver Burdett Press, 1990.

CRITICISM AND REVIEWS OF INDIVIDUAL VOLUMES

I Know Why the Caged Bird Sings

Arensberg, Liliane K. "Death as Metaphor of Self in *I Know Why the Caged Bird Sings*." *College Language Association Journal* 20 (1976): 273–96.

Article on *Caged Bird*. http://www.planetout.com/pno/newsplanet/article.html/1998/01/13/4.

Demetrakopoulous, Stephanie A. "The Metaphysics of Matrilinearism in Women's Autobiography: Studies of Mead's *Blackberry Winter*, Hellman's *Pentimento*, Angelou's *I Know Why the Caged Bird Sings*, and Kingston's *The Woman Warrior*." In *Women's Autobiography: Essays in Criticism*. Ed. Estelle Jelinek. Bloomington: Indiana University Press, 1980. 180–205.

Gross, R. A. "Growing Up Black." Rev. of *I Know Why the Caged Bird Sings*. *Newsweek* 2 Mar. 1970: 90–91.

Guiney, E. M. Rev. of *I Know Why the Caged Bird Sings*. *Library Journal* 16 Mar. 1970: 1018.

Lehmann-Haupt, Christopher. "Books of the Times: Masculine and Feminine." Rev. of *I Know Why the Caged Bird Sings*. *New York Times* 25 Feb. 1970: 45.

Minudri, Regina. Rev. of *I Know Why the Caged Bird Sings*. *Library Journal* 15 June 1970: 2320.

Smith, Sidonie Ann. "The Song of a Caged Bird: Maya Angelou's Quest after Self-Acceptance." *Southern Humanities Review* 7 (1973): 365–75.

Sutherland, Zena. Rev. of *I Know Why the Caged Bird Sings*. *Saturday Review* 9 May 1970: 70.

Vermillion, Mary. "Reembodying the Self: Representations of Rape in *Incidents in the Life of a Slave Girl* and *I Know Why the Caged Bird Sings*." *Biography* 15 (1992): 243–60.

Gather Together in My Name

Adams, Phoebe. Rev. of *Gather Together in My Name*. *Atlantic* June 1974: 233.

Almeida, Ruth E. Rev. of *Gather Together in My Name*. *Library Journal* 1 June 1974: 1538.

Bloom, Lynn Z. "Maya Angelou." *Dictionary of Literary Biography*. Vol. 38. Detroit: Gale, 1985. 3–12.

Cudjoe, Selwyn R. "Maya Angelou and the Autobiographical Statement." In *Black Women Writers (1950–1980): A Critical Evaluation*. Ed. Mari Evans. Garden City, NY: Doubleday, 1984. 6–24.

———. "Maya Angelou: The Autobiographical Statement Updated." In *Reading Black, Reading Feminist*. Ed. Henry Louis Gates Jr. New York: Penguin, 1990. 272–306.

Gottlieb, Annie. Rev. of *Gather Together in My Name*. *New York Times Book Review* 16 June 1974: 87.

Minudri, Regina. Rev. of *Gather Together in My Name*. *Library Journal* 15 May 1974: 99.

Rev. of *Gather Together in My Name*. *New Republic* 16 July 1974: 32.

Sukenick, Lynn. Rev. of *Gather Together in My Name*. *Village Voice* 11 July 1974: 31.

Singin' and Swingin' and Gettin' Merry Like Christmas

Jordan, June. Rev. of *Singin' and Swingin' and Gettin' Merry Like Christmas*. *Ms.* Jan. 1977: 40–41.

Kuehl, Linda. Rev. of *Singin' and Swingin' and Gettin' Merry Like Christmas*. *Saturday Review* 30 Oct. 1976: 46.

Mitchell, Lisa. "Maya Angelou: Sometimes She Feels Like a Motherless Child." Rev. of *Singin' and Swingin' and Gettin' Merry Like Christmas*. *Los Angeles Times* 21 Nov. 1976: 5.

Robinson, Kathryn. Rev. of *Singin' and Swingin' and Gettin' Merry Like Christmas*. *Southern Literary Journal* Summer 1976: 144.

The Heart of a Woman

Cosgrave, M. S. Rev. of *The Heart of a Woman*. *Horn Book* Feb. 1982: 84.

Lewis, David Levering. "A Transitional Time: *The Heart of a Woman*." In *Readings on Maya Angelou*. San Diego, CA: Greenhaven, 1997. 152–55.

Neubauer, Carol E. "Displacement and Autobiographical Style in Maya Angelou's *The Heart of a Woman*." *Black American Literature Forum* 17 (1983): 123–29.

Pascal, Sylvia. Rev. of *The Heart of a Woman*. *Southern Literary Journal* Dec. 1981: 88.

Rev. of *The Heart of a Woman*. *Choice* Jan. 1982: 621.

Spigner, Nieda. Rev. of *The Heart of a Woman*. *Freedomways* 1 (1982): 55.

All God's Children Need Traveling Shoes

Baker, Houston. Rev. of *All God's Children Need Traveling Shoes*. *New York Times Book Review* 11 May 1986: 14.

Blundell, Janet Boyarin. Rev. of *All God's Children Need Traveling Shoes*. *Library Journal* 15 Mar. 1986: 64.

Gropman, Jackie. Rev. of *All God's Children Need Traveling Shoes*. *Southern Literary Journal* Aug. 1986: 113.

Gruesser, John C. "Afro-American Travel Literature and Africanist Discourse." *Black American Literature Forum* 24 (1990): 5–20.

McDowell, Deborah E. "Traveling Hopefully." *The Women's Review of Books* 4 (October 1986): 17.

Rev. of *All God's Children Need Traveling Shoes*. *Time* 31 Mar. 1986: 72.

OTHER SECONDARY SOURCES

Abrams, M. H. *A Glossary of Literary Terms*. 6th ed. New York: Harcourt, 1993.

Anderson, Jervis. *This Was Harlem*. New York: Farrar, 1981.

Andrews, William L. *To Tell a Free Story: The First Century of Afro-American Autobiography: 1760–1865*. Urbana: University of Illinois Press, 1986.

Black Elk. *Black Elk Speaks*. 1932. Ed. John Neihardt. New York: Pocket Books, 1972.

Braxton, Joanne M. *Black Women Writing Autobiography: A Tradition Within a Tradition*. Philadelphia, PA: Temple University Press, 1989.

Brent, Linda (Harriet Jacobs). *Incidents in the Life of a Slave Girl*. 1861. New York: Harcourt, 1973.

Brooks, Gwendolyn. *Report from Part One*. Detroit: Broadside, 1972.

Burgher, Mary. "Images of Self and Race in the Autobiographies of Black Women." In *Sturdy Black Bridges*. Ed. Roseann P. Bell, Bettye J. Parker, and Beverly Guy-Sheftall. Garden City, NY: Doubleday, 1979. 107–22.

Butterfield, Stephen. *Black Autobiography in America*. Amherst: University of Massachusetts Press, 1974.

Carby, Hazel V. *Reconstructing Womanhood: The Emergence of the Afro-American Woman Novelist*. New York: Oxford University Press, 1987.

Carson, Benjamin S. *Gifted Hands: The Ben Carson Story*. New York: HarperCollins, 1993.

Dance, Daryl C. "Black Eve or Madonna?" In *Sturdy Black Bridges*. Ed. Roseann P. Bell, Bettye J. Parker, and Beverly Guy-Sheftall. Garden City, NY: Doubleday, 1979. 123–32.

Davis, Angela. *Angela Davis*. New York: Random House, 1974.

Douglass, Frederick. *Narrative of the Life of Frederick Douglass*. 1845. In *The Classic Slave Narratives*, ed. Henry Louis Gates Jr. New York: New American Library, 1987.

Encarta. CD-Rom. Microsoft: Multimedia Encyclopedia. 1994.

Equiano, Oloudah. *Gustavus Vassa, the African, or the Interesting Narrative of the Life of Olaudah Equiano.* 1789, 1814. In *The Classic Slave Narratives*, ed. Henry Louis Gates Jr. New York: New American Library, 1987.

Fleischner, Jennifer. *Mastering Slavery.* New York: New York University Press, 1996.

Fox-Genovese, Elizabeth. "Myth and History: Discourse of Origins in Zora Neale Hurston and Maya Angelou." *Black American Literature Forum* 24 (1990): 221–56.

Froula, Christine. "The Daughter's Seduction: Sexual Violence and Literary History." *Signs* 114 (1986):621–44.

Gates, Henry Louis, Jr. "The Blackness of Blackness: A Critique of the Sign of the Signifying Monkey." In *Black Literature and Literary Theory.* Ed. Henry Louis Gates Jr. New York: Methuen, 1984. 285–321.

———. *Colored Pople.* New York: Vintage, 1995.

———. *The Signifying Monkey: A Theory of African-American Literary Criticism.* New York: Oxford University Press, 1988.

Giovanni, Nikki. *Gemini: an extended autobiographical statement on my first twenty-five years of being a black poet.* Indianapolis: Bobbs-Merrill, 1971.

Golden, Marita. *Migrations of the Heart.* 1983. New York: Ballantine Books, 1987.

Gross, Leslie. "Parent Calls Required Book Explicit, Racially Divisive." *The Capital* (27 October 1997):A1, A10.

Harmon, William, and C. Hugh Holman. *A Handbook to Literature.* 7th ed. Upper Saddle River, NJ: Prentice-Hall, 1996.

Hellman, Lillian. *Pentimento.* Boston: Little, Brown, 1973.

Hemenway, Robert E. *Zora Neale Hurston.* Urbana: University of Illinois Press, 1977.

Hill-Lubin, Mildred A. "The Grandmother in African and African-American Literature: A Survivor of the Extended Family." In *Ngambika: Studies of Women in African Literature.* Ed. Carole B. Davies and Anne A. Graves. Trenton, NJ: Africa World, 1986. 257–70.

Hirsch, Marianne. "Maternal Narratives: 'Cruel Enough to Stop the Blood.' " In *Reading Black, Reading Feminist.* Ed. Henry Louis Gates Jr. New York: Penguin, 1990. 415–30.

———. *The Mother/Daughter Plot.* Bloomington: Indiana University Press, 1989.

Holly, Carol T. "*Black Elk Speaks* and the Making of Indian Autobiography." *Genre XII* (spring 1979):117–36.

Homer. *The Odyssey: Book XI.* In *The Norton Anthology of World Masterpieces*, vol. 1. Ed. Maynard Mack. New York: Norton, 1995. 332–48.

hooks, bell. *Bone Black: Memories of Girlhood.* New York: Holt, 1996.

Howarth, William L. "Some Principles of Autobiography." 1974. In *Autobiography.* Ed. James Olney. Princeton: Princeton University Press, 1990. 84–114.

Hughes, Langston. "The Big Sea." 1940. In *Bearing Witness.* Ed. Henry Louis Gates Jr. New York: Pantheon Books, 1991. 64–78.

———. "Feet Live Their Own Life." In *The Best of Simple*. 1961. New York: Farrar, Straus & Giroux, 1989.

Hurston, Zora Neale. *Dust Tracks on a Road*. 1942. Ed. Robert E. Hemenway. Urbana: University of Illinois Press, 1984.

———. *Their Eyes Were Watching God*. 1937. Urbana: University of Illinois Press, 1978.

Johnson, Georgia Douglas. "The Heart of a Woman." In *The Heart of a Woman* (1918). Reprinted in *No More Masks*. Ed. Florence Howe. New York: HarperCollins, 1993.

Johnson, James Weldon. "Go Down Death—A Funeral Sermon." In *God's Trombones: Seven Negro Sermons in Verse*. New York: Viking, 1966.

Jones, LeRoi. *Blues People*. New York: Morrow, 1963.

Kazin, Alfred. "Autobiography as Narrative." *Michigan Quarterly Review* 3 (fall 1964):210–16.

Lessing, Doris. *Under My Skin*. New York: HarperCollins, 1994.

———. *Walking in the Shade*. New York: HarperCollins, 1994.

Malcolm X. *The Autobiography of Malcolm X: With the Assistance of Alex Haley*. New York: Grove Press, 1965.

Mandel, Barrett J. "The Autobiographer's Art." *Journal of Aesthetics and Art Criticism* 27 (winter 1968):216–26.

Marshall, Paule. *Praisesong for the Widow*. New York: E. P. Dutton, 1984.

Mason, Mary G. "Travel as Metaphor and Reality in Afro-American Women's Fiction." *Black American Literature Forum* 24 (1990):337–56.

McBride, James. *The Color of Water*. New York: Riverhead Books, 1996.

McDowell, Deborah E. "In the First Place: Making Frederick Douglass and the Afro-American Tradition." In *African American Autobiography*. Ed. William L. Andrews. Englewood Cliffs, NJ: Prentice-Hall, 1993. 36–58.

McKay, Claude. "If We Must Die." In *Selected Poems of Claude McKay*. New York: Bookman Associates, 1953.

Moody, Anne. *Coming of Age in Mississippi*. New York: Dell Publishing, 1968.

Moore, Gerald, and Ulli Beier, eds. *The Penguin Book of Modern African Poetry*. London: Penguin Books, 1968.

The Norton Anthology of African American Literature. Ed. Henry Louis Gates Jr. and Nellie Y. McKay. New York: Norton, 1997.

Olney James. "Autobiography and the Cultural Moment: A Thematic, Historical, and Bibliographical Introduction." In *Autobiography: Essays Theoretical and Critical*. Ed. James Olney. Princeton: Princeton University Press, 1980.

———, ed. *Autobiography: Essays Theoretical and Critical*. Princeton: Princeton University Press, 1980.

The Oxford Companion to African American Literature. Ed. William L. Andrews, Frances Smith Foster, and Trudier Harris. New York: Oxford University Press, 1997.

"Parents Say Maya Angelou Poem too Graphic for Youngsters." *Black News Today*

(September 1997):1–2. http://www.blackvoices.com/news/97/09/12/ story02.htm/

Pascal, Roy. *Design and Truth in Autobiography*. Cambridge, MA: Harvard University Press, 1960.

Ramsey, R. Priscilla. "Transcendence: The Poetry of Maya Angelou." *A Current Bibliography on African Affairs* 17 (1984–85): 139–53.

Sayre, Robert F. "Autobiography and the Making of America." In *Autobiography*. Ed. James Olney. Princeton: Princeton University Press, 1980. 146–68.

Shelton, Austin, ed. *The African Assertion: A Critical Anthology of African Literature*. New York: Odyssey, 1968.

Southern, Eileen. *The Music of Black Americans: A History*. New York: Norton, 1971.

Stein, Gertrude. *The Autobiography of Alice B. Toklas*. 1933. New York: Vintage Books, 1960.

Tierney, Helen, ed. *Women's Studies Encyclopedia*. 1989. New York: Peter Bedrick, 1991.

Walker, Alice. *The Color Purple*. New York: Harcourt Brace Jovanovitch, 1982.

———. *In Search of Our Mother's Gardens: Womanist Prose*. 1967. New York: Harcourt, 1983.

Weixlmann, Joel. "African American Autobiography: A Bibliographical Essay." *Black American Literature Forum* 24 (1990): 375–415.

Wright, Elizabeth, ed. *Feminism and Psychoanalysis: A Critical Dictionary*. Oxford: Blackwell, 1992.

Wright, Richard. *American Hunger*. 1944. New York: Harper & Row, 1979.

———. *Black Boy*. Cleveland: World, 1945.

Wright, Sarah. *This Child's Gonna Live*. 1986. New York: Feminist Press at The City University of New York.

Index

About the Author

MARY JANE LUPTON is professor of English at Morgan State University in Baltimore, Maryland. A founder of *Women: A Journal of Liberation*, she was one of the co-editors of this Baltimore-based magazine from 1970 to 1984. The author of numerous articles on African American literature, she is co-author, with Emily Toth and Janice Delaney, of *The Curse: A Cultural History of Menstruation* (1976 and 1989). She is also author of a ground-breaking book, *Menstruation and Psychoanalysis* (1993).

Critical Companions to Popular Contemporary Writers
Kathleen Gregory Klein, Series Editor

V. C. Andrews
by E. D. Huntley

Tom Clancy
by Helen S. Garson

Mary Higgins Clark
by Linda C. Pelzer

Arthur C. Clarke
by Robin Anne Reid

James Clavell
by Gina Macdonald

Pat Conroy
by Landon C. Burns

Robin Cook
by Lorena Laura Stookey

Michael Crichton
by Elizabeth A. Trembley

Howard Fast
by Andrew Macdonald

Ken Follett
by Richard C. Turner

Ernest J. Gaines
by Karen Carmean

John Grisham
by Mary Beth Pringle

James Herriot
by Michael J. Rossi

Tony Hillerman
by John M. Reilly

John Irving
by Josie P. Campbell

John Jakes
by Mary Ellen Jones

Stephen King
by Sharon A. Russell

Dean Koontz
by Joan G. Kotker

Robert Ludlum
by Gina Macdonald

Anne McCaffrey
by Robin Roberts

Colleen McCullough
by Mary Jean DeMarr

James A. Michener
by Marilyn S. Severson

Toni Morrison
by Missy Dehn Kubitschek

Anne Rice
by Jennifer Smith

Tom Robbins
*by Catherine E. Hoyser and
Lorena Laura Stookey*

John Saul
by Paul Bail

Erich Segal
by Linda C. Pelzer

Amy Tan
by E. D. Huntley

Anne Tyler
by Paul Bail

Leon Uris
by Kathleen Shine Cain

Gore Vidal
by Susan Baker and Curtis S. Gibson